S0-AKK-774

Santa Cruz
A GUIDE FOR RUNNERS, JOGGERS AND SERIOUS WALKERS

We welcome your comments and suggestions.

Santa Cruz is a dynamic and changing community. New parks are being opened and new trails developed. We want to make sure we keep this guide useful, accurate and up-to-date, and we would appreciate any comments or suggestions that would help us improve future editions of this book.

Please send your comments to:

Editorial Department
Journeyworks Publishing
P.O. Box 8466
Santa Cruz, CA 95061-8466

Or email: editorial@journeyworks.com

Thanks!

Santa Cruz
A GUIDE FOR RUNNERS, JOGGERS AND SERIOUS WALKERS

Eileen Brown
and
Steven Bignell

Journeyworks Publishing
Santa Cruz, California

© 2005 Journeyworks Publishing
All rights reserved. No part of this book may be reproduced, transmitted or otherwise used in any form or by any means, electronic, mechanical or otherwise, including but not limited to photocopying or by means of any information storage and retrieval system, without express written permission from the publisher. Requests for permission should be made in writing to Journeyworks Publishing, P.O. Box 8466, Santa Cruz, CA 95061-8466.

Maps by Dale Nutley, Grendel Design
Graphic Design by Eva Bernstein

Cover photo of Judith & Julia running in Pogonip by Ben Hewlett

Other Photo Credits:
Ben Hewlett, pp 8
John Hilmer, pp 82
Ron Austin, pp 88
All other photos by the authors.

ISBN 1-56885-397-1

Manufactured in the United States of America
Published by: Journeyworks Publishing
P.O. Box 8466
Santa Cruz, CA 95061-8466
831-423-1400   Fax 831-423-8102
Editorial @journeyworks.com
www.journeyworks.com

An Important Caution to Our Readers

Readers must assume personal responsibility for their safety and security when running or walking the routes described in this book and should exercise appropriate caution and common sense.

The authors and Journeyworks Publishing assume no liability for damage or loss arising from errors or omissions, if any, in this book, and are not responsible for accidents, incidents, personal injuries, damage to property or any other losses sustained by readers who engage in the activities described in this book.

This book is sold without warranties or guarantees of any kind, express or implied, and the authors and publisher disclaimer any liability, loss or damage caused by the contents.

If you do not wish to be bound by these cautions and conditions, disagree with the foregoing disclaimer of liability, you may return this book for a full refund of the purchase price.

Dedicated to:

Daniel Brown

Joel Brown

Alex Bignell

Maggie Bignell

TABLE OF CONTENTS

see page 14

see page 30

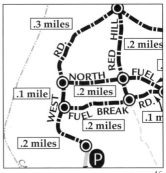

see page 46

see page 74

POPULAR RACE ROUTES

see page 82

MILEAGE MAPS FOR SANTA CRUZ NEIGHBORHOODS

APPENDICES

see page 92

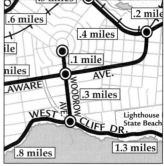

see page 98

see page 101

Courtesy Ben Hewlett

ACKNOWLEDGEMENTS

Not only are we fortunate to live in an area with wonderful places to walk and run, we are especially fortunate to live in a town full of generous, creative and talented people. This book could not have been written without their help.

One of the most formidable tasks in developing this book was the need to create clear, simple and accurate maps. Dale Nutley of Grendel Design was the perfect choice for us. He has a fine eye and exceptional patience. The incomparable Eva Bernstein, whose style and speed is unmatched in this profession, provided the book and cover designs. And major thanks to Mardi Richmond, senior editor at Journeyworks, for her valiant efforts in trying to keep us organized and moving forward, as well as for writing the section "Running or Walking with Your Dog."

We would like to express our thanks to the Santa Cruz Track Club for the loan of the wheel used to measure the accuracy of these courses, the use of race photographs and general helpfulness. The staffs of the City of Santa Cruz Department of Parks and Recreation, the County of Santa Cruz Department of Parks and Open Spaces, the California State Parks Department, and the Land Trust of Santa Cruz County were very helpful in compiling maps and information.

Thanks to Maria Waddell, Erica Aiken, Carol Cuminale, Sue Potter, Anne Stafford, Kate Clark, Judith Carey, Rachel Glassberg and Karen Warren for their invaluable feedback on the manuscript.

We both want to thank our respective spouses, Neil Brown and Mary Bignell, for their love, support and commitment to us and our kids.

Eileen would also like to thank members of the Ryan's Sports Shop racing team 1985–2000 who introduced her to most of the trail running in Santa Cruz county and supported her in her love of running, especially Gail and Gary Goettlemann, Laura Sanchez, Karen Schulte, John and Sandy Sup, Tina and Rich McCandless, Juana Stavalone, Kristen Jacobs, Dave and Terri LaBerge, Mike and Sue Cronk, Dave Davis, Barry Farrara, Rosa Gutierrez and Barb Myers-Acosta.

Steven also wants to thank his regular running partner Doug Kirby, whose intellect and conversation keeps the miles moving swiftly even if we aren't. And he must mention Dennis, Jonathan, Victor, Andy, Colin and Rick, who, although they had absolutely nothing to do with this book, deserve all the attention they can get.

The late Donald Thomas Clark, whose seminal reference work, *Santa Cruz County Place Names*, provided many of the historical facts we have interspersed throughout the text, deserves special mention. His book is one that everyone interested in Santa Cruz history should have as part of their personal library.

INTRODUCTION

Our primary goal in writing this book is to provide you with descriptions and mileage maps of running and walking routes around the greater Santa Cruz area. We hope to encourage you to get out and explore our beautiful parks, beaches and neighborhoods – and to get some serious exercise while doing so. Because most people like the satisfaction of knowing how far (and perhaps how fast) they have run or walked, we have included accurate and detailed mileage for all the routes described. Each loop and trail was measured with a transit wheel, often more than once, to achieve accurate and up-to-date mileage.

How to Use This Book

We have divided the route descriptions into sections. The first part of the book describes neighborhood routes and loops while the second part lists trails within our parks. Within each section we've organized the routes in a roughly north to south and west to east order as they curve around the bay. Our descriptions are short and simple, providing you with a little history, an overall sense of the distance and difficulty of each route or trail, and a brief overview of the features of the route. A short section on safety is followed by *Other Things You Should Know*, describing parking, restroom, water fountain or other information. Each description has an accompanying map showing the routes/trails and providing detailed mileage indicators.

The first section, **NEIGHBORHOOD ROUTES AND LOOPS**, describes running and walking areas in and around various residential neighborhoods. These routes are great for local residents who just want to walk out their front door and get some exercise but are also interesting for those who want to experience other parts of Santa Cruz. Some of the routes include the coastal bluff neighborhoods of *West Cliff, Seabright, Pleasure Point*, and *Rio Del Mar*; the neighborhoods of *West Lake* and *Prospect Heights* with their expansive views; and the uniquely scenic *Santa Cruz Yacht Harbor* and *San Lorenzo River Levee*.

We've grouped state, county and city park trails into our **PARKS AND GREENBELT** section. Santa Cruz County has parks and great diversity of scenery, with hundreds of beautiful trails from which to choose. We obviously couldn't describe them all, so in selecting trails for this book, we've chosen those which are most suitable for running and serious walking – trails that are scenic and interesting, have good footing, and which have, for the most part, year around accessibility. In addition to the well known parks such as *Wilder Ranch, Henry Cowell* and *The Forest of Nisene Marks*, we've included lesser known parks such as *DeLaveaga, Schwan Lake* and *Anna Jean Cummings*. We've included both easy trails for walkers and beginning runners and long, steep trails for serious runners and hikers.

Since you can't talk about running or walking in Santa Cruz without mentioning our **BEACHES**, we've also included short descriptions and mileage maps of some of the longer and more popular beaches for walking and running.

POPULAR RACE ROUTES provides descriptions and course maps with mileage for some of Santa Cruz's great races, including the internationally known *Wharf to Wharf*, the always popular *Turkey Trot* and *Firecracker 10k*, and the oldest cross country race still going on in Santa Cruz, the *Cardiac Pacer*. Looking forward to a race is an excellent motivator and a good way to set a goal. We are lucky in Santa Cruz to have fun races that attract runners of all ages and abilities.

Recognizing that many people like to jog in and around their neighborhood and would like to be able to estimate the distance they have run, we have included a section called **MILEAGE MAPS FOR SANTA CRUZ NEIGHBORHOODS** which highlights key streets with distances marked. If you run on a nearby street, the mileage will help you estimate the length of your specific run.

The **APPENDICES** also include suggestions for *Running or Walking on the Track*, *Running Indoors at Santa Cruz Gyms*, *Safety Tips*, a *Pacing Chart*, a section on *Running or Walking with Your Dog* and a *Running Route Checklist* to help you keep track of how many different routes (and total miles) you've run.

A note about mileage indicators on the maps:

A few of our trail measurements are not the same as on other published maps or on trail marker signs. Those routes were checked and rechecked with a transit wheel. We have noted when our calculations have differed from others. Of course, trail wash outs and other changes can always affect routes and mileage.

> **"**I always loved running...it was something you could do by yourself, and under your own power. You could go in any direction, fast or slow as you wanted, fighting the wind if you felt like it, seeking out new sights just on the strength of your feet and the courage of your lungs.**"**
> – **Jesse Owens**

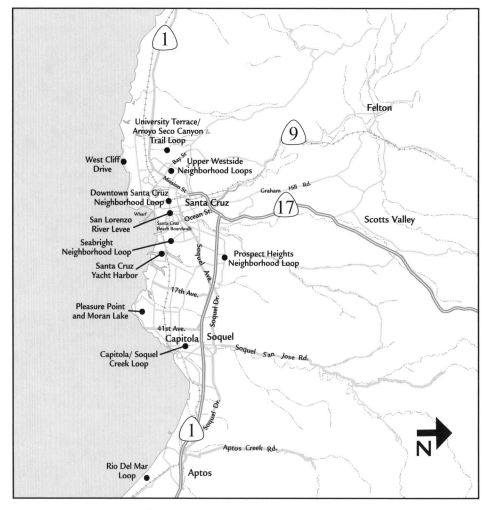

SANTA CRUZ:
A GUIDE FOR RUNNERS, JOGGERS AND SERIOUS WALKERS

NEIGHBORHOOD ROUTES AND LOOPS

WEST CLIFF DRIVE

West Cliff Drive is considered one of the premier running and walking routes in Santa Cruz. Its long, paved stretch passes by Steamer Lane, Lighthouse Point, dozens of million dollar homes and miles of crashing surf. Steamer Lane, named for the steamer ship traffic that used to travel between San Francisco and Los Angeles, is a world-renowned surfing spot just off Lighthouse Point. Lighthouse Field State Beach includes 40 acres of undeveloped headlands, the Mark Abbott Memorial Lighthouse and the Surfing Museum. According to local historian Ross Eric Gibson, Santa Cruz was once called the "Newport of the Pacific" because the row of mansions along West Cliff Drive resembled Newport, Rhode Island.

Route and Features

You can start at virtually any point along West Cliff Drive. If you begin at the corner of Bay and West Cliff, you will run .6 of a mile to the lighthouse. Through this stretch you will be treated to the sight of wetsuit-clad surfers enjoying Steamer Lane. You will also pass the 18-foot tall bronze statue of a surfer guarding the lane. Sculpted by Thomas Marsh and Brian W. Curtis and completed in 1991, it quickly became a local landmark. When the weather is clear, the view of the Santa Cruz Mountains from this part of West Cliff is spectacular.

As you travel the 1.9 miles between Lighthouse Point and Natural Bridges State Beach, you are heading to the northwest tip of Monterey Bay where it begins to join the ocean. In late winter and early spring, migrating whales are often sighted along this stretch as they travel between Mexico and Alaska.

The onshore sea breezes along West Cliff can be quite strong, and on windy days you may want to plan your return run to be heading from Natural Bridges towards the lighthouse so that the wind is at your back.

Distance and Difficulty

This 5 mile round trip route is flat, paved, and perfect for runners of all ages and abilities. Because of its proximity to the ocean, running or walking along West Cliff Drive on warm days can be refreshingly cool while foggy days can be wet and cold.

Safety

The biggest danger along West Cliff Drive is running into someone. West Cliff is popular with runners, bicyclists, people on roller blades, parents with strollers, and people walking dogs. Especially on weekends, stay alert for others in your path.

Other Things You Should Know

There are restrooms and drinking fountains at Lighthouse Field State Beach. If you run all the way into Natural Bridges State Park, you will also find restrooms and water fountains at the entrance to the beach and at the visitor center.

Parking is available in lots along West Cliff Drive and on side streets. Summer weekends can be very busy and it may be difficult to park.

WEST CLIFF DRIVE

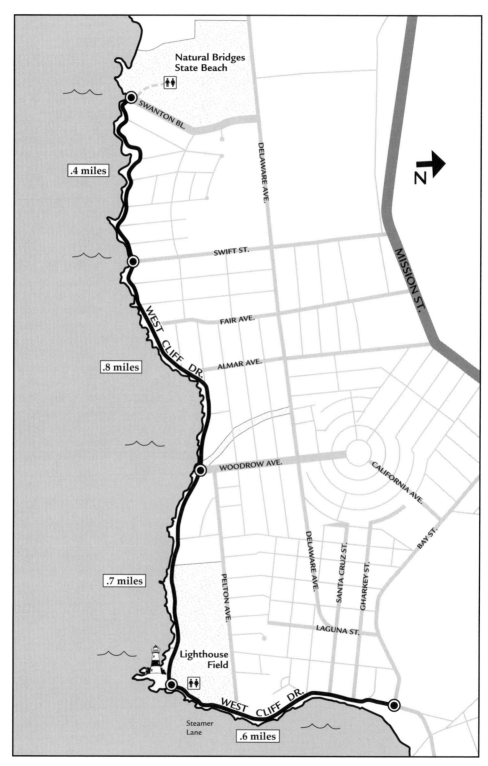

Natural Bridges
State Beach

SWANTON BL.

.4 miles

DELAWARE AVE.

MISSION ST.

SWIFT ST.

WEST CLIFF DR.

FAIR AVE.

.8 miles

ALMAR AVE.

WOODROW AVE.

CALIFORNIA AVE.

DELAWARE AVE.

SANTA CRUZ ST.

GHARKEY ST.

BAY ST.

.7 miles

PELTON AVE.

LAGUNA ST.

Lighthouse
Field

WEST CLIFF DR.

Steamer
Lane

.6 miles

UNIVERSITY TERRACE/ARROYO SECO CANYON TRAIL LOOP

Neighborhood streets and a quiet canyon trail combine to make this a unique loop. It features the Arroyo Seco Canyon Trail, a steep, isolated path in a deep canyon between residential neighborhoods. The canyon is home to rabbits, deer and a large number of birds. Depending on the direction you choose, you will either run down the steep canyon path and climb the hills of Alta Vista and Nobel Drive or run down the steep streets and up the path. The name University Terrace reflects the step-like terraces on which the homes in this area are built. From an aerial view, the terraces look like giant steps leading from the ocean up to the university.

Route and Features

The entrance to Arroyo Seco Canyon Trail is easy to spot from Meder Street. At the far right side of University Terrace Park you will see an asphalt service road. It is paved for the first few hundred yards and then becomes a gravel trail. Follow it 1.1 miles down to the bottom of the canyon. At the bottom you will cross two small bridges shortly before the trail becomes a narrow path. The path runs along a chain-link fence until it ends at Grandview Avenue. Turn left on Grandview and left again onto Escalona. Then turn left up the steep hill onto Arroyo Seco Drive and begin your climb. At the top of the hill, turn right onto Alta Vista Drive. Between houses you can see some great views of west Santa Cruz. Follow Alta Vista as it curves to the left and continue until it ends at Nobel Drive. Turn left on Nobel. Notice the street signs as you run along Nobel Drive: they are named after University of California professors who have won the Nobel Prize. Some people think the street layout resembles a strand of DNA. Continue on Nobel Drive back to Meder Street.

It is a little difficult to spot the entrance to the canyon if you are entering from Grandview Street. About 15 yards west of the intersection of Grandview Street and Escalona, look for the small park with a sign that says "Private for members of the Santa Cruz Mission Apartments only." On the right hand side of the park you will see a small path bordered by a low chain-link fence running behind the apartments. Follow the path for about 80 yards, go across the little wooden bridge, and you have entered Arroyo Seco Canyon.

Distance and Difficulty

Portions of this 2.5-mile loop are quite steep (especially the residential stretch between Escalona and Nobel).

Safety

The canyon is isolated. Homes are barely visible and high above you. While some cyclists, walkers and runners do use the path, often you will not see another person. You might want to consider running with a partner. The run consists of steep hills, which can be slippery, especially in the winter when fallen leaves, puddles and muddy runoff cover much of the canyon trail.

Other Things You Should Know

University Terrace Park is located in the upper Westside of Santa Cruz on Meder Street between Bay Street and Western Drive.

There is plenty of street parking available along the residential parts of the route and next to University Terrace Park. There is water but no restroom at the park.

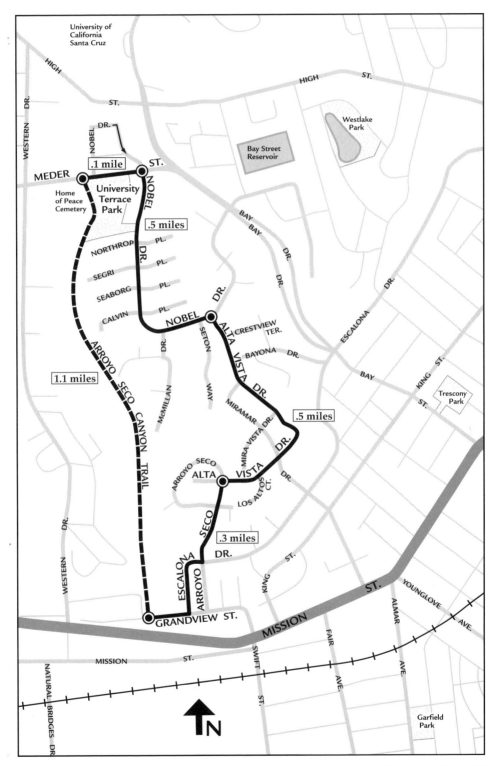

UPPER WESTSIDE NEIGHBORHOOD LOOPS

You can choose between an easy flat loop or a challenging hilly loop on these two upper Westside neighborhood routes. The upper Westside is characterized by a series of giant steps or terraces, with steep to moderate climbs connecting them. Escalona Drive is in the middle of two of these terraces. (*Escalona* is the Spanish word for "steps" or "stairs.") The varying architectural styles of the homes adds to the enjoyment of running along these residential streets.

Route and Features

Escalona Drive/King Street Loop

The Escalona/King Street loop is relatively flat and easy to follow. While you can begin your run or walk at any point, for ease of description we begin at the corner of Highland Avenue and Escalona Drive. From here proceed west on Escalona, which runs at a mild incline to Bay Street. Follow Escalona across Bay Street until it curves down and intersects Baldwin Street. Head straight on Baldwin to King Street and turn left. At the end of King, turn left onto Mission Street for a short distance to reach Highland Avenue and return to Escalona. King Street, east of Bay, can be busy with traffic. You can turn off King Street at any time and travel up one of the many intersecting streets to return to Escalona for a quieter and slightly steeper run.

High Street Loop

An alternative loop begins at the same corner of Escalona and Highland. Proceed up Highland Avenue to High Street. Except during times of busy university traffic in the early morning and late afternoon, High Street is quiet. The sidewalk is primarily just on the downhill side of High Street and is narrow in places. You will climb up a long hill for most of your run to Bay Drive. Turn left at Bay Drive for a downhill return to Escalona. On Bay, after Nobel Drive, the sidewalks disappear and you will have to run on the wide shoulder. You can also take the bike/pedestrian path that runs along the center median of Bay Drive (between Nobel Drive and Escalona), although the path is hidden and isolated from view. The significant feature of this loop, other than the long hill climb, is the spectacular view of the Monterey Bay.

Distance and Difficulty

Escalona/King Street Loop
A mostly flat 2.3-mile loop

High Street Loop
A moderately difficult 3-mile loop with long uphill and downhill stretches.

Safety

You will need to cross many busy intersections and where there are no sidewalks, be aware of traffic. Lighting at night is limited.

Other Things You Should Know

There are no public bathrooms or water fountains anywhere on the route. You can park on the streets in most areas, but permit parking is needed closer to the university.

UPPER WESTSIDE NEIGHBORHOOD LOOPS

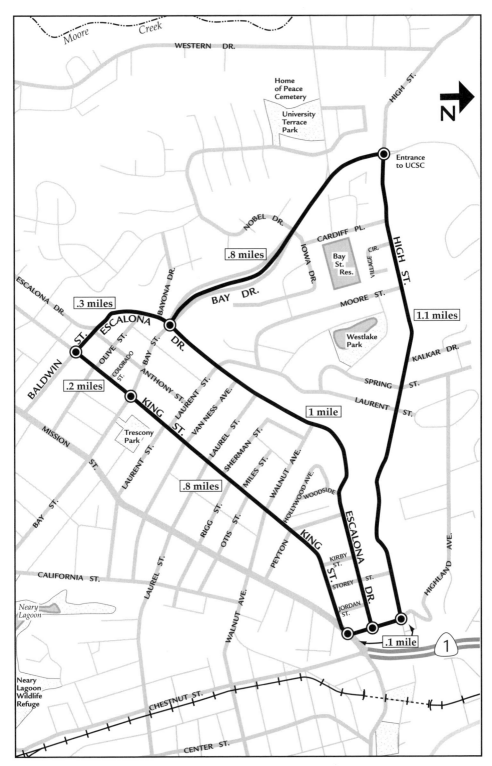

DOWNTOWN SANTA CRUZ NEIGHBORHOOD LOOP

An interesting downtown loop is the old race course of the City of Santa Cruz Five-Miler. Though the race was discontinued in 2003 due to lack of funding, the course provides a wonderful tour of the main features of Santa Cruz. It begins in the downtown shopping district on Pacific Avenue, passing Santa Cruz High School and Neary Lagoon on its way to the beachfront. You will run past the Santa Cruz Beach Boardwalk and onto the San Lorenzo River levee before finishing back downtown.

Route and Features

The loop begins at the corner of Pacific and Lincoln Streets in downtown Santa Cruz. Leaving downtown, you head straight uphill on Lincoln, merge with Walnut Street and pass Santa Cruz High School. Turn left onto California Street. Proceed on California past Laurel Street and turn left when you reach Bay Street. Bay Street takes you past Neary Lagoon and the water treatment facility as you head toward the ocean. Turn left down Beach Street past the wharf, Santa Cruz Main Beach and the Santa Cruz Beach Boardwalk. At the end of Beach Street you will intersect with Third Street. Follow it around to the left. When you reach the Riverside Street bridge, cross over to your right onto Third Street. Third Street takes you through Beach Hill and past some of the grand old homes of Santa Cruz's past and present. Make a hairpin turn onto Front Street and head back towards downtown. Continue on Front Street and make a right onto Laurel Street Extension. When you get to the San Lorenzo River levee, go left and run along the levee to the Water Street bridge. To complete the loop follow River and Front Street once again around the post office to Santa Cruz's main shopping and entertainment area, Pacific Avenue.

Distance and Difficulty

An easy to moderate 5-mile loop with a few hills.

Safety

The loop is recommended during non-business hours, as it would be hard to run down Pacific Avenue when shops and businesses are open. The San Lorenzo River levee is fairly isolated and is a regular spot for illegal camping. You might want to consider running with someone. Follow the map carefully if you are not familiar with the Beach Hill/levee area as it can be confusing.

Other Things You Should Know

You can park anywhere along the route. Be sure to feed the meters if necessary, as the Santa Cruz meter readers are very diligent. There is also plenty of free parking available. Water and restrooms can be found at the Main Beach as well as downtown.

DOWNTOWN SANTA CRUZ NEIGHBORHOOD LOOP

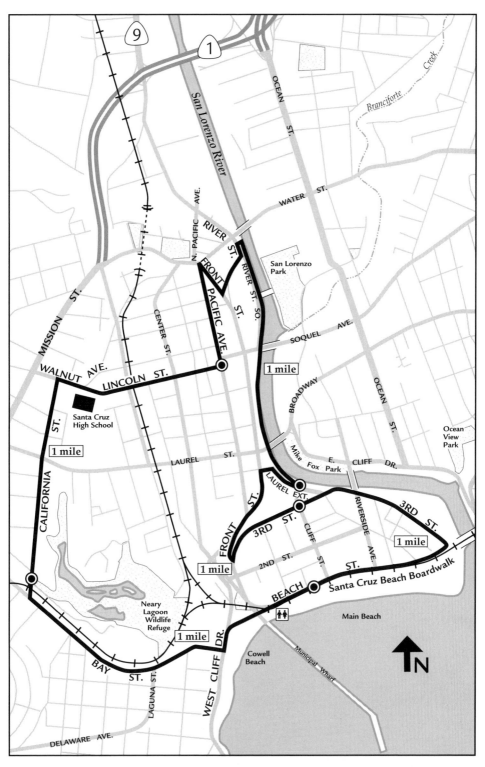

SAN LORENZO RIVER LEVEE

The asphalt bike and pedestrian path along the top of the San Lorenzo River Levee provides a quiet, uncrowded and scenic route through the heart of downtown Santa Cruz. The scenery along this route changes dramatically with the tides and seasons. Ducks, geese, herons and other migrating birds add to the interest along the river.

The San Lorenzo River runs 22 miles from the Santa Cruz Mountains to the Monterey Bay. First seen by Europeans from the Portola Expedition of 1769, the San Lorenzo was named in honor of Saint Lawrence, a third-century Christian martyr. The San Lorenzo River is considered the dividing line between the East and West sides of Santa Cruz.

After the extensive December floods of 1955, the Army Corp of Engineers built the levee to protect downtown Santa Cruz from future flooding. The levee was redesigned and reinforced in 2000 and now includes a bike and foot path. The path runs from the San Lorenzo River mouth (near the Santa Cruz Beach Boardwalk) along both sides of the San Lorenzo River to Highway 1.

Route and Features

You can start the run anywhere along the length of the levee. If you start on the east side near the train trestle, you'll run on the sidewalk along East Cliff Drive for about 250 yards before the levee begins. Continue on the levee, passing under the Riverside and Laurel Street bridges until the levee path ends briefly at the Soquel Avenue bridge. Crossing Soquel Avenue you rejoin the path in San Lorenzo Park and travel under the Water Street bridge until the levee path ends at Highway 1. Because there is no pedestrian crossing on the Highway 1 bridge, you will need to backtrack and cross over on the Water Street bridge. To run the full route, head up the other side of the levee to Highway 1 and then return back to continue along the west side of the levee. You will again pass under the bridges, this time on the west side. Continue on the levee to the train trestle next to the Boardwalk, where you can cross over to complete the loop.

Distance and Difficulty

A 4.7-mile flat, easy loop. Shorter loops can be run by crossing any one of four bridges.

Safety

Watch out for bicyclists, particularly on the narrow bridge underpasses. The riverbank area is a scenic and quiet area to run, but it is also fairly isolated and a regular spot for illegal camping. You might want to consider running with a partner. The levee path is only open during daylight hours.

Other Things You Should Know

Restrooms and water fountains along the route are in San Lorenzo Park near the lawn bowling courts. Restrooms in the Boardwalk parking lot are open during Boardwalk business hours.

Free parking is available in the lots on Front Street between Laurel and Water Streets, with metered parking along the street next to San Lorenzo Park.

SAN LORENZO RIVER LEVEE

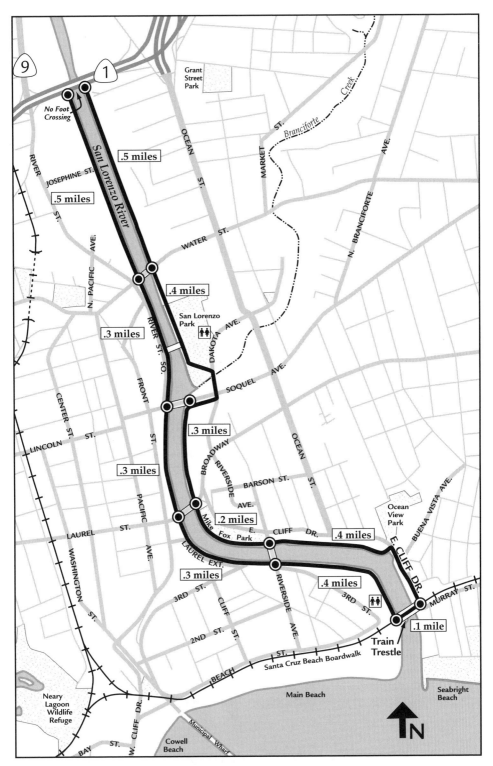

SEABRIGHT NEIGHBORHOOD LOOP

A scenic mix of neighborhood streets, beach, cliffs and the harbor make for an inviting run for locals and non-locals alike. Seabright is generally defined as the area south of Soquel Avenue and bordered by Ocean View Avenue, the harbor, and the beach. Begun as a summer colony, Seabright once had its own post office and rail-road station. Families from the Central Valley and Sacramento built cottages and bungalows here to escape the summer heat. Mott Street is named after the original owner of the land, F.M. Mott, who developed and named the area in the 1880's. Seabright Beach is also known as Castle Beach because of the castle-like structure that stood at the entrance to the beach from 1899 until it was demolished in 1967.

Route and Features

You can begin this route at many places. One common starting point is the "five corners." This is the neighborhood name for the intersection of Pine, Cayuga, Clinton and Buena Vista, centrally located in the Seabright neighborhood. If you start here, proceed down Buena Vista Avenue to East Cliff Drive. Cross East Cliff and turn to your left. You will see the Southern Pacific Railroad trestle to your right as you cross high above the tracks. The Santa Cruz Beach Boardwalk can be seen across the river to your right.

Turn right on East Cliff and follow it to the entrance of Seabright Beach. You can take a detour and add to your run by going onto the beach and running to the jetty. (See page 78 for this beach run.) Otherwise continue on East Cliff a half block past the Seabright Beach entrance to Seabright Avenue. Turn right on Seabright towards the bay, then turn left onto the pedestrian path along the cliffs. Take the pedestrian path to 4th Avenue, go up 4th and turn right onto Atlantic. At Mariner Park Way turn left down into the Yacht Harbor parking area. As you descend the hill you can enjoy a spectacular view of the Santa Cruz Mountains in the background and the blue-covered sails of the boats in the foreground. Continue around the harbor. About 500 yards past the Murray-Eaton Street bridge, you'll come to stairs on your left which lead to Frederick Street Park and a completed loop down Windham Street back to Cayuga Street.

For a slightly shorter route you can begin at the intersection of Seabright Avenue and Murray Street. You proceed straight down Seabright to the beach overlook, turn left along the cliffs and continue to the harbor. You may want to return to this starting point to enjoy the great food and drinks available at the establishments in Seabright Junction.

Distance and Difficulty

A flat 3-mile loop for all levels of runners.

Safety

Much of this route is traffic-free along the cliffs and through the harbor. It is well used by walkers and runners. Caution is needed at the crossing of East Cliff Drive near the railroad trestle. There is no crosswalk and traffic comes around a blind curve. Some summer weekends can get quite busy through a small stretch of the harbor, but there is plenty of room to avoid the sailboats being hoisted into the water.

Other Things You Should Know

Restrooms and drinking fountains are available at Seabright Beach, the harbor and Frederick Street Park. You can park on the street throughout the neighborhood, with a few exceptions. Parking is regulated by permit in the summer on and around Buena Vista. Check for posted signs. There is metered parking at the harbor.

SEABRIGHT NEIGHBORHOOD LOOP

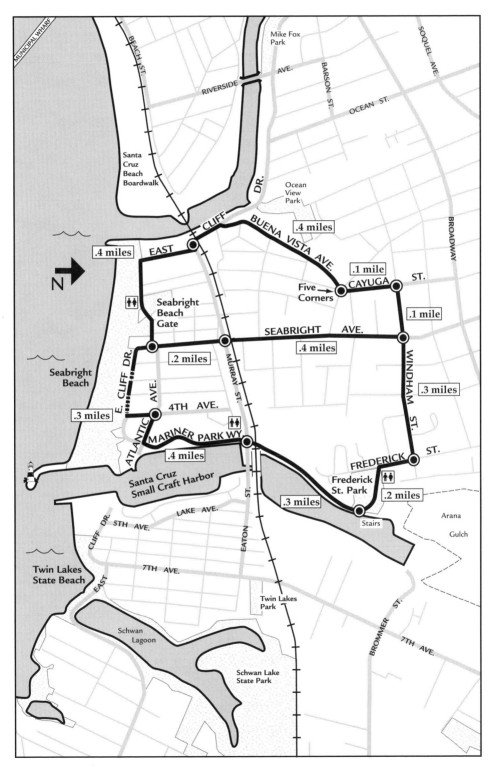

PROSPECT HEIGHTS NEIGHBORHOOD LOOP

This neighborhood loop features flat paved roads and sidewalks with a short trail option. Prospect Heights is a neighborhood sandwiched between Highway 1 and DeLaveaga Golf Course. In the 1920's Prospect Heights was part of Chickentown, which spanned the area from DeLaveaga to Live Oak and was named for the large number of chicken farms in the area. The two large palm trees at DeLaveaga School originally flanked the entrance to one of the largest farms. DeLaveaga School, built in 1967, sits in the center of the neighborhood.

Route and Features

You can begin anywhere on this loop. If you begin in front of DeLaveaga School, proceed around the school west on Prospect Heights to DeLaveaga Park Road. You will run through the neighborhood past homes and churches. Where Prospect Heights joins DeLaveaga Park Road, you'll see a stone entrance gatepost which still remains from the mansion which stood here, a remnant of the grand days of the area. After DeLaveaga Park Road intersects North Branciforte, you will head back along Goss Avenue, Rooney Street, and Morrissey Boulevard. This part of the loop is on paved streets and sidewalks and has low traffic except during the morning and afternoon rush hour when commuters avoiding Highway 1 often use Rooney Street. Once you return to DeLaveaga School, you will have gone 2 miles. To continue the full loop, go east on Prospect Heights to Brookwood Drive and veer left up the only steep hill on the loop. Near the top of the hill is a gate. If it is locked to traffic, you can step through the pedestrian gate and continue uphill. Although the gate has a sign warning of the archery and shooting range, you will be turning well before the range. At the fork, take the road to your left. After about 50 yards take the dirt road on your left, passing a large water tank on the hill above to your right. The dirt road will lead you along the hillside behind homes and back to Park Way, where you will go around the chain gate. Turn left on Prospect Heights to complete the figure 8 loop.

Distance and Difficulty

This 3.3-mile figure 8 loop is mainly flat and paved with one steep hill and a .4-mile unpaved stretch. It is appropriate for all levels. You can also shorten it to a 2-mile loop.

Safety

Most of the first part of the loop, along paved streets and sidewalks, is lit by streetlights at night. The dirt road on the longer route is flat and in good condition, though it can be slippery after rain. It is somewhat isolated but is in sight of backyards.

Other Things You Should Know

There are no restrooms or water. You can park on the street throughout the neighborhood.

PROSPECT HEIGHTS NEIGHBORHOOD LOOP

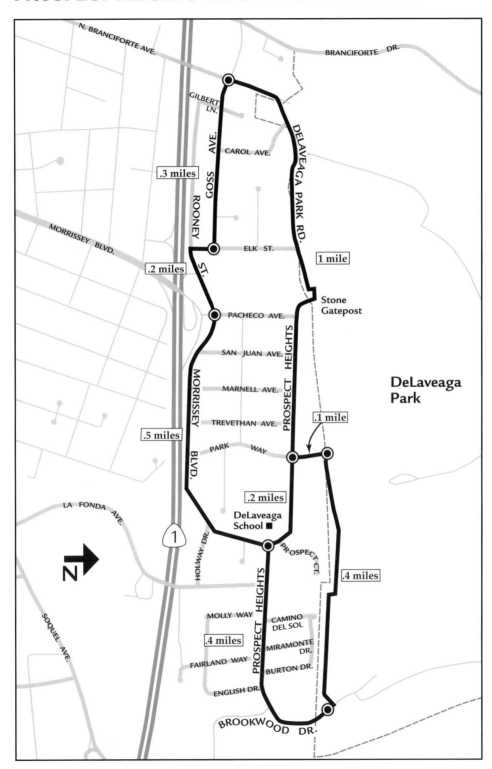

SANTA CRUZ YACHT HARBOR

Devoid of cross streets and neighborhood traffic, and relatively quiet on weekdays, this area is a popular route for both runners and bicyclists. On windy or stormy days it allows you to run near the water while being protected from the fiercest of the elements. The route affords great views of boats entering the harbor mouth or settled into their berths. You may also see an occasional sea lion swimming near the mouth or basking on the rocks and, if you run early, commercial and sport fishermen unloading their daily catch.

The Santa Cruz Yacht Harbor (officially the Santa Cruz Small Craft Harbor) was built on the site of the former Woods Lagoon in 1963. Expanded in 1973, the yacht harbor has over 900 berths housing everything from small sailboats to ocean-going yachts. The Glenn Coolidge Memorial Bridge, which divides the upper from the lower harbor, was named after Assemblyman Glenn E. Coolidge. He was instrumental in establishing the small craft harbor and bringing UCSC to Santa Cruz. A new lighthouse was dedicated in 2002 at the end of the jetty overlooking the harbor mouth.

Route and Features

The route is flat and asphalt or sidewalk for its entire length. If you start out at the Crow's Nest restaurant near the mouth of the harbor, you first take the sidewalk path along the edge of the harbor parking lot toward the Glenn Coolidge Bridge. When you reach the end of the parking lot, go up the hill, turn left and follow the path under the bridge. You continue up and around the end of the upper harbor and then return on the west side of the harbor back under the bridge, down past Aldo's Restaurant and out onto the jetty. Your total distance one way is 1.9 miles. You can always shorten the route (or your return) by crossing the Glenn Coolidge Bridge. (There is a stairway up the west side of the yacht harbor to the bridge.)

The west side of the harbor can be reached by turning east on Atlantic Avenue off of Seabright Avenue. The east side of the harbor can be reached by turning south onto Lake Avenue off of Eaton Street. You can enter the upper harbor directly off of 7th Avenue at Brommer Street. There is metered or fee parking in all of the harbor parking lots. There is free on-street parking next to Twin Lakes Beach, except on summer weekends when it is regulated by permit. There is also parking on the streets near Aldo's Restaurant.

Distance and Difficulty

This flat out and back run covers 3.8 miles. It can be shortened in either or both directions by going up and over the bridge.

Safety

This is an active harbor. Boats are launched on both sides and there is commercial activity on the east side. The yacht harbor can be especially busy on weekends, and since sidewalks around the harbor are narrow, you may find yourself darting into the parking lot to pass walkers. The path is narrow as it passes under the bridge, and there is a blind curve. Harbor vehicles and bikes use this path along with runners and walkers. The jetty near the lighthouse is often wet and can get slippery.

Other Things You Should Know

There are public restrooms near the Crow's Nest, in the Upper Harbor near the RV parking area, behind the Chardonnay office just under the west side of the bridge, and by the boat hoist near the west entrance. The restrooms immediately adjacent to the docks are for the use of boat owners and are usually locked.

SANTA CRUZ YACHT HARBOR

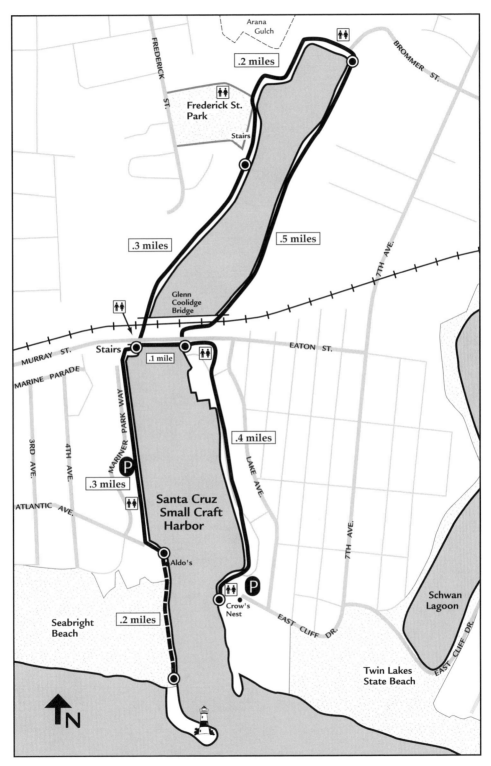

.2 miles

Arana Gulch

FREDERICK ST.

BROMMER ST.

Frederick St. Park

Stairs

.3 miles

.5 miles

7TH AVE.

Glenn Coolidge Bridge

Stairs

MURRAY ST.

EATON ST.

.1 mile

MARINE PARADE

MARINER PARK WAY

.4 miles

LAKE AVE.

3RD AVE.

4TH AVE.

P

.3 miles

Santa Cruz Small Craft Harbor

ATLANTIC AVE.

7TH AVE.

Aldo's

P

Crow's Nest

EAST CLIFF DR.

Schwan Lagoon

Seabright Beach

.2 miles

Twin Lakes State Beach

EAST CLIFF DR.

N

PLEASURE POINT AND MORAN LAKE

This scenic loop combines ocean cliffs, a quiet lakeside trail and a run through part of the quaint beachside neighborhood of Pleasure Point. Originally known as Soquel Point, Pleasure Point is one of the county's prime surfing spots, and the beautiful scenery makes this an especially enjoyable run. The loop includes Moran Lake Park, a 9.2-acre regional park encompassing a small beach, lake and picnic area.

Route and Features

A good place to start this loop is at the small park (officially, 41st Avenue County Park) at the end of 41st Avenue where it intersects East Cliff Drive. This surfing area is also known as The Hook. Here you'll find a parking lot, restroom and a few picnic tables overlooking the surfers below. Run southwest along East Cliff, enjoying the ocean view while avoiding bicycles and strollers. You will run past a knoll with benches. Just past Palisades Avenue, you will see a stand of eucalyptus trees. Veer right here onto Moran Way and follow the paved path to your left as it curves down to Moran Lake Park. You will briefly rejoin East Cliff Drive as the path crosses in front of the lake. Turn right into the parking area. Run along the trail next to Moran Lake as it slowly climbs a narrowing gully. Although homes will be visible on both sides, the trail is covered in a canopy of trees and has a quiet, secluded feel. After a half mile you'll reach the end of the trail, where you can either reverse your route and head back, or continue up to the right, following a narrow path next to an apartment complex, until you reach 30th Avenue. Turn right on 30th, and after a few hundred yards turn right again onto Scriver Avenue. Make the second left onto Palisades and take it all the way back to East Cliff Drive. As you run along Scriver and Palisades, check out the interesting homes in the neighborhood. At East Cliff, turn left and retrace your steps .7 miles back to 41st Avenue.

Check out the Live Oak/Pleasure Point mileage map on page 100 or the Wharf to Wharf map on page 83 for information on extending your run down East Cliff Drive.

Distance and Difficulty

This is a mostly flat 2.4-mile loop. The majority of the run is on pavement with a .5-mile stretch of wood chip and dirt trail along Moran Lake.

Safety

Use appropriate caution as you will be sharing this busy route with bicycles, strollers and people walking dogs. Some stretches of this route have no sidewalks. Portions of the Moran Lake trail are secluded. You may want to run this section with a friend.

Other Things You Should Know

Public restrooms, water fountains and parking can be found at both Moran Lake Park and 41st Avenue Park. East Cliff Drive is one way from 32nd Avenue to 41st due to oceanside erosion. Summer weekends are very crowded and parking is difficult to find.

PLEASURE POINT AND MORAN LAKE

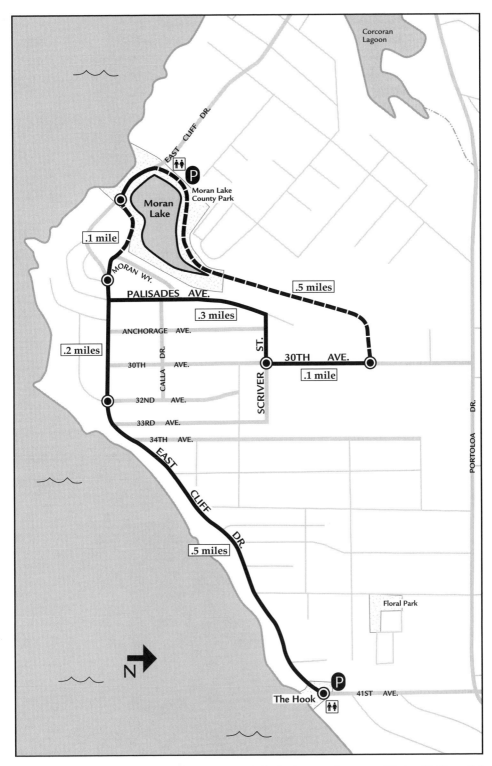

Corcoran Lagoon

EAST CLIFF DR.

Moran Lake County Park

Moran Lake

.1 mile

MORAN WY.

PALISADES AVE.

.5 miles

.3 miles

ANCHORAGE AVE.

CALLA DR.

SCRIVER ST.

.2 miles

30TH AVE.

30TH AVE.

.1 mile

32ND AVE.

33RD AVE.

34TH AVE.

EAST CLIFF DR.

PORTOLOA DR.

.5 miles

Floral Park

N

The Hook

41ST AVE.

CAPITOLA/SOQUEL CREEK LOOP

This short loop features a footpath, bike path, sidewalks, hills and flat stretches, views of the bay and a close up look at Soquel Creek and its wildlife. It also passes by the Rispin Mansion. Henry Allen Rispin built the 22-room mansion in the 1920's, when he owned much of Capitola, including a hotel, a tent city, and a bathhouse. The City of Capitola purchased the Rispin Mansion in 1985. The city had hoped to use the mansion and land for a community center, library or park, although at the time of this writing, plans call for it to become a bed and breakfast.

Route and Features

The asphalt path begins behind Nob Hill Foods parking lot on Bay Avenue in Capitola. Park in the very back of the parking lot and you will see the path climbing up in front of you. The path will take you to a bridge crossing Soquel Creek. After crossing the bridge, the path winds past the Rispin Mansion to Wharf Road, where you will turn left and run on sidewalks and along the shoulder. Just past the Shadowbrook Restaurant, you will head downhill, going under the train trestle. When you get to Cliff Drive, turn left and cross the Stockton Avenue bridge. Immediately after crossing the bridge, turn left and go down to the path alongside the creek. This dirt and sand path leads you along a pedestrian right-of-way through the backyards of summer cottages and year-round homes that line Soquel Creek. Where the path ends, turn left on Riverview Avenue and follow it to Riverview Drive. Turn left again to return to your starting point.

Distance and Difficulty

A flat 1.6-mile loop on pavement and sidewalks.

Safety

The loop is in view of traffic and homes, with the exception of the short bike path which climbs past Rispin Mansion. Most of the run is along paths or sidewalks.

Other Things You Should Know

There are public restrooms, a water fountain and parking in the rear of the Nob Hill lot.

CAPITOLA/SOQUEL CREEK LOOP

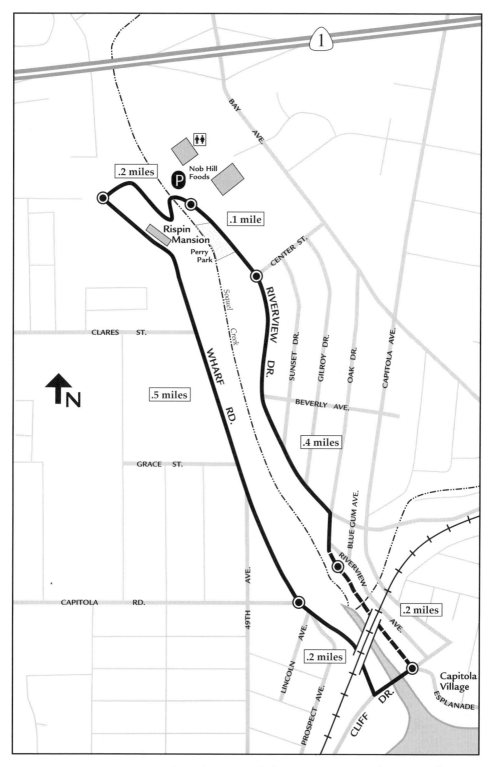

RIO DEL MAR LOOP

Rio Del Mar was once part of Rafael Castro's vast Rancho Aptos estate, which encompassed most of the coast between what is now Cabrillo College and La Selva Beach. In 1872 the land around Rio Del Mar was purchased by Claus Spreckels, the famous sugar baron. In the 1920's, after Spreckels' death, the land was given the name Rio Del Mar (River of the Sea) by land developers. Rio Del Mar is now a neighborhood of year-round homes and summer rentals. It consists of the "flats" along Aptos Creek, the beachfront, and the cliff neighborhood between the railroad tracks and the ocean.

While many people drive to Rio Del Mar to run on the beach or along the walkway to the cement ship, this loop offers an alternative through scenic beach neighborhoods. This loop is an especially good option when the tide is too high for beach running or you want a bit longer run than the walkway provides.

Route and Features

Beginning at the Rio Del Mar esplanade, run up the steep hill on Rio Del Mar Boulevard to Cliff Drive. While Cliff Drive is flat, wide and easy to run, we suggest taking the less-traveled side streets of Kingsbury, Seaview and Bayview Drive. Each of these streets winds through the cliff-side neighborhood before returning to Cliff Drive a few blocks later. Seaview gives you a view of the bay and pedestrian access to the beach. A quick descent down Cliff Drive dead ends at Hidden Beach Park, where you can continue further on the beach or complete the loop with a beach run back to the esplanade. If you prefer to stay on the roads, return via Townsend Drive. Turn left onto Kingsbury Drive and right onto Cliff Drive until you merge again with Rio Del Mar Boulevard. The fabulous view of Seacliff State Beach rewards you on the final downhill back to the start.

Also see page 79 for a mileage map of New Brighton and Seacliff State Beaches.

Distance and Difficulty

A mostly flat 3.1-mile loop with steep hills at the beginning and end of the route.

Safety

There are no sidewalks on this loop. Care must be taken running along the shoulder of Cliff Drive as it is a well-used main street.

Other Things You Should Know

There are restrooms and water where the loop begins and ends at the esplanade.

RIO DEL MAR LOOP

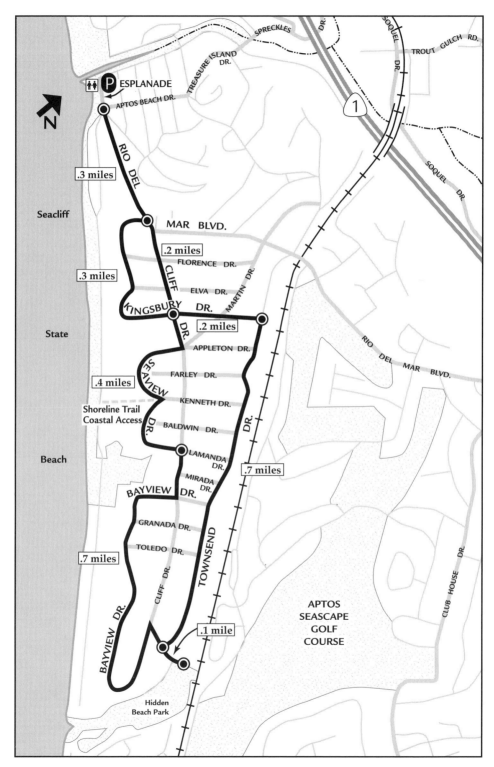

ESPLANADE

TREASURE ISLAND DR.

SPRECKLES DR.

TROUT GULCH RD.

SOQUEL DR.

1

SOQUEL DR.

APTOS BEACH DR.

RIO DEL

.3 miles

Seacliff

MAR BLVD.

.2 miles

FLORENCE DR.

MARTIN DR.

.3 miles

CLIFF DR.

ELVA DR.

KINGSBURY DR.

State

.2 miles

APPLETON DR.

RIO DEL MAR BLVD.

SEAVIEW DR.

FARLEY DR.

.4 miles

KENNETH DR.

Shoreline Trail
Coastal Access

BALDWIN DR.

Beach

LAMANDA DR.

.7 miles

MIRADA DR.

BAYVIEW DR.

TOWNSEND DR.

GRANADA DR.

.7 miles

TOLEDO DR.

CLIFF DR.

APTOS
SEASCAPE
GOLF
COURSE

CLUB HOUSE DR.

.1 mile

BAYVIEW DR.

Hidden
Beach Park

"*Climb the mountains and get their good tidings. Nature's peace will flow into you as sunshine flows into trees. The winds will blow their own freshness into you, and the storms their energy, while cares will drop away from you like the leaves of Autumn.***"**

– John Muir

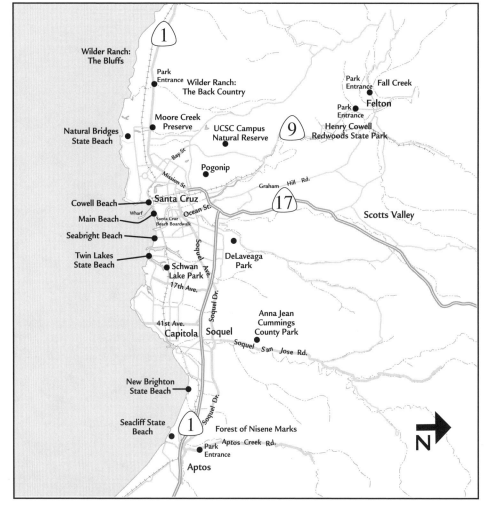

SANTA CRUZ:
A GUIDE FOR RUNNERS, JOGGERS AND SERIOUS WALKERS
· ·

PARKS AND GREENBELT

WILDER RANCH STATE PARK:
THE BLUFFS

The flat, wide bluffs trails at Wilder Ranch are among the most beautiful spots to run or walk in the county. The trail winds along cliffs just above the ocean with views of rocky out-crops, crashing waves and blue, green and turquoise coves. Bird life is abundant, and the colors of wildflowers in the spring and summer add to the beauty. You'll also see farm fields and the hills of Wilder Ranch, which was originally the main rancho supplying food to the mission at Santa Cruz. The ranch later became a very successful dairy farm and then a vegetable farm. In 1974 Wilder Ranch was purchased by the State of California, preserving the land from development. Now a state park, the ranch has a restored central area with farmhouse, bunkhouse and barns. The pedestrian roadway in front of the main house is the original Highway 1.

Route and Features
Old Cove Landing Trail

This trail begins at the edge of the state park parking lot. With the restrooms on your left, look toward your right for the dirt path that crosses the railroad tracks. There are no cross trails, turns or forks on this path. Just follow the trail which is completely flat and wide for its full length. At 1.25 miles you will encounter Sand Plant Beach. You can turn back here or make a shorter loop run by continuing around the farm field to your right. This trail leads you along a private farm road, across the railroad tracks and back to the entrance station in the parking lot.

Ohlone Bluff Trail

At Sand Plant Beach the Old Cove Landing Trail becomes the Ohlone Bluff Trail. Head down the rocky trail, cross the beach and climb up the trail on the other side. The footing is good and the trail well marked on both sides of the beach crossings. At times, high tide may make the beach crossing difficult. You can loop around the lagoon by following the trail to the right at the beach trail marker. Turn left at the railroad tracks and run alongside the tracks to the next field, where you turn left again and follow the first dirt road to rejoin the Ohlone Bluff Trail. The trail terrain is a soft but stable dirt road with plenty of passing room. Weekdays and Saturdays may find farm activity in the adjoining fields, but Sundays are quiet. The Ohlone Bluff Trail passes Strawberry Beach, Three Mile Beach and Four Mile Beach. The state park maps show the trail continuing under Highway 1 to meet with the Baldwin Creek trail in the back country. Because the trail is difficult to follow past Four Mile Beach, we suggest you turn back here.

There is beach access from the Ohlone Bluff Trail to Four Mile Beach, and there are restrooms but no water fountains located at the beach entrance.

Distance and Difficulty
Old Cove Landing Trail
A very easy, completely flat 2.5-mile out-and-back trail or 2-mile loop.

Ohlone Bluff Trail
A 7-mile, very easy, completely flat out-and-back addition to the Old Cove Landing Trail (for a total run of 9.5 miles).

Safety
The trails travel along sheer cliffs where signs warn visitors to keep back from the edge. Cyclists, hikers and runners all share the same trail. While the wind is cooling, the bluffs are exposed to the sun with no shade.

Other Things You Should Know
A 1.25-mile bike path links Santa Cruz to Wilder Ranch State Park. Park at the intersection of Shaffer Road and Highway 1 and follow the bike path until it ends at the rear of the ranch buildings.

There is a large parking lot inside the state park. Fees are collected as you enter. You can also park free at the pull-out on the side of Highway 1. Restrooms and water fountains are available in the parking lot.

WILDER RANCH STATE PARK: THE BLUFFS

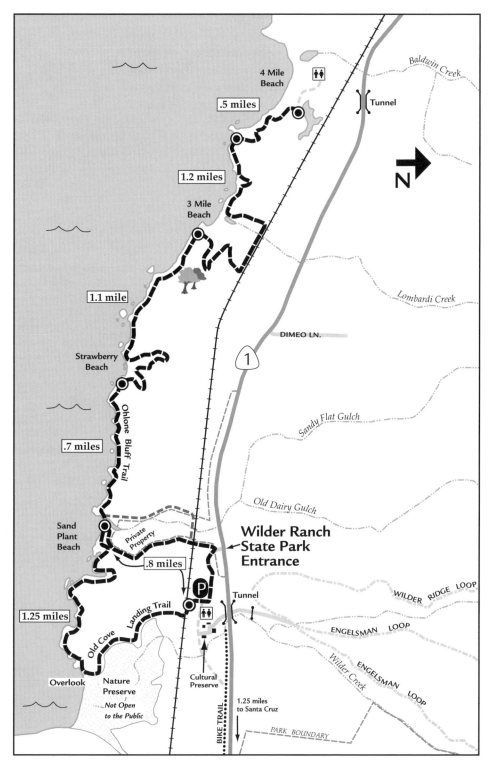

4 Mile Beach

.5 miles

Tunnel

Baldwin Creek

N

1.2 miles

3 Mile Beach

Lombardi Creek

1.1 mile

DIMEO LN.

1

Strawberry Beach

Sandy Flat Gulch

Ohlone Bluff Trail

.7 miles

Old Dairy Gulch

Sand Plant Beach

Private Property

Wilder Ranch State Park Entrance

.8 miles

WILDER RIDGE LOOP

1.25 miles

Landing Trail

Tunnel

ENGELSMAN LOOP

Old Cove

ENGELSMAN LOOP

Overlook

Nature Preserve

Not Open to the Public

Cultural Preserve

Wilder Creek

1.25 miles to Santa Cruz

BIKE TRAIL

PARK BOUNDARY

WILDER RANCH STATE PARK:
THE BACKCOUNTRY

The backcountry of Wilder Ranch offers varying terrain, elevation changes and views of the redwoods and the ocean. The former Grey Whale Ranch is a recent addition to state park land, and a complete trail now connects the ocean to the redwood-covered Santa Cruz Mountains.

Route and Features

To reach the backcountry, go past the ranch buildings through the tunnel under Highway 1. A cow gate and a large trail map sign 200 yards in front of you designate the beginning of the backcountry. Most of these trails are exposed to the sun with very little shade, climbing from sea level to elevations of 800 feet. Footing is usually good with occasional patches of gravel.

The Englesman Loop

The Englesman Loop begins just past the entrance to the backcountry. Take the dirt road straight past the horse corral to the trail marker. The loop consists of a wide dirt road for its entire length. Starting with the right fork, climb up for 1.4 miles, turn left at the trail intersection at the top, and run back down for 1.6 miles. You will pass through open meadow with no shade but with great views of the backcountry and ocean.

The Wilder Ridge Loop

The Wilder Ridge Loop trail is a moderate to difficult run consisting of steep hills, wide dirt roads, and single-track trails. It passes through meadows, around ponds, through scrubby manzanita growth and under live oak trees. Most of the trail is exposed to sun.

The trailhead is found 100 yards past the entrance to the backcountry. After passing the horse corral on your right, take the left fork of the dirt road and continue 50 yards to the hairpin turn on your left, where you will see the marker for the Wilder Ridge Trail. The trail begins with a .3-mile long steep uphill climb. At .7 miles, turn left on the single-track trail. There is a trail marker here. The trail climbs up and down small hills as it winds around gullies and usually dry streams. This section of the trail has both deep sandy spots and hard boulder crossings, but for the most part it is hard packed dirt with a few roots.

At 2.4 miles the trail for the Zane Grey cutoff heads to the right. The Wilder Ridge Loop continues down and to your left. It passes through a boggy area which can be very wet in the winter, then turns right and follows alongside a horse ranch and the city dump. At the top of the long climb, you come to the intersection of many trails. Bear to your right up the rocky dirt road to continue on the Wilder Ridge Loop trail, which is well marked. The trail widens at this point, where you run along the flat ridge top before beginning a long, steep downhill back to the trailhead. (continued on page 43)

Distance and Difficulty

Englesman Loop
Moderate 3.1-mile trail, half uphill and half downhill.

Wilder Ridge Loop
6.9 miles of moderate to strenuous running.

Eucalyptus Loop
A 7.6-mile loop covering much of the ranch, featuring a wide dirt road, single-track trails, meadows and woods. The footing ranges from dirt to rocky but is good in most places.

Enchanted Loop
A 1.6-mile extension to the Eucalyptus or Wilder Ridge Loops.

Long Meadow Loop
A 5.8-mile extension to the Chinquapin Trail, best accessed from the UCSC Campus Natural Reserve.

WILDER RANCH STATE PARK: THE BACKCOUNTRY

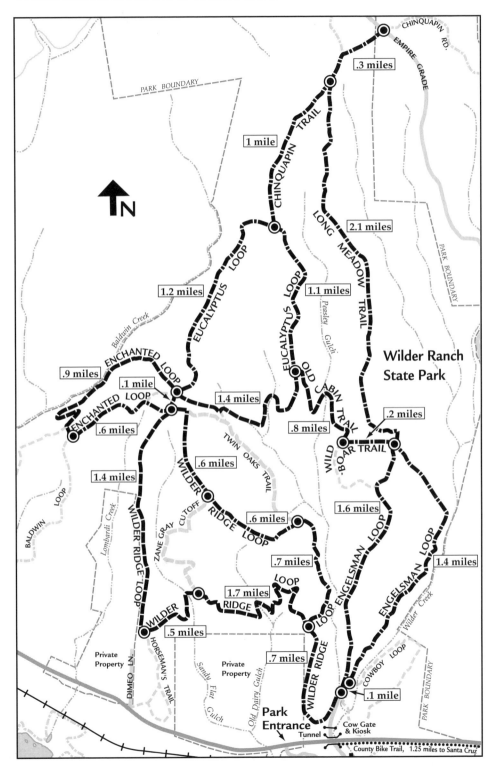

Above: Traveling along Wilder Ridge Loop.

Below: Historic buildings in the cultural preserve.

Eucalyptus Loop

Take the Englesman Loop 1.4 miles to the intersection of the Wild Boar Trail and continue straight ahead onto this trail. After .2 miles on the Wild Boar Trail you'll join the Old Cabin Trail for .8 miles. This one-mile section of the loop is single-track through the trees. The footing is good as it climbs down and back up crossing a usually dry creek at the bottom. The shade is welcome on a warm day. The Old Cabin Trail connects to the Eucalyptus Loop. Turn right at the intersection with the Eucalyptus Loop and climb through the meadow to the top of the state park and the eucalyptus grove. From this spot, enjoy the panoramic view of the entire park and the Pacific Ocean beyond. Continue on the Eucalyptus Loop to the bottom. Turn left and run a short distance on asphalt until you come to the intersection of several trails. Turn left again to return to the start via the Wilder Ridge Loop.

Enchanted Loop

Just past the top of the Wilder Ridge Loop and intersecting with the Eucalyptus Loop is the Enchanted Loop Trail. This trail truly feels enchanted. It runs under towering redwoods, alongside a falling creek and past a fern grotto. It is one of the most magical trails at Wilder and well worth the extra miles.

Long Meadow Loop

Runners enjoying the trails at the UCSC Campus Natural Reserve (see page 46) can extend their run by connecting with the Long Meadow Loop in the upper reaches of Wilder Ranch. This 5.8-mile loop begins at Chinquapin Trail, where it crosses Empire Grade Road and enters Wilder Ranch. The unpaved Chinquapin Trail connects with the Long Meadow Trail, which descends gradually but continuously through wide-open meadow on a very wide trail. The footing is good although steep in a few places and there is no shade. At the bottom of the trail you will pass the lime kilns which were active in this area during the 1920's. Turn right and pass through the opening in the fence to the intersection with the Englesman Loop. Turn right at this intersection onto the Wild Boar Trail. Follow it to the Old Cabin Trail, and then turn right at the Eucalyptus Loop. Run 1.1 miles to the intersection with the Chinquapin Trail. The Chinquapin Trail is a flat wide dirt road which can be rutted in places. It runs through meadow and low shrubs back to UCSC.

Safety

These are multi-use trails. Wilder Ranch is one of the few parks in the county that allows mountain bikes full trail access. It is accepted local courtesy to give mountain bikes the right of way. Mountain bikes move fast, so beware as you traverse these trails, especially on weekends. Caution is also needed in passing horses on the trail. Always check with the rider for permission to pass.

This is also mountain lion country. Read the signs so you are aware of what to do if you encounter a mountain lion. The backcountry trails are isolated and exposed and can be very hot. We recommend that you carry water on sunny days.

Other Things You Should Know

There is a large parking lot inside the state park. Fees are collected as you enter. Restrooms and water fountains are available in the parking lot and near the ranch buildings. There is no water available in the backcountry.

MOORE CREEK PRESERVE

Opened in the spring of 2003, Moore Creek Preserve is the newest addition to the greenbelt surrounding the City of Santa Cruz. Formerly known as the Bombay Property, it was at the center of numerous court battles concerning its development. The city acquired the property in 1998 and manages it together with the Land Trust of Santa Cruz County. The preserve is filled with wildflowers, wildlife and spectacular views of the ocean. At this time, however, the trails are quite limited.

Routes and Features

Prairie View/Terrace Loop Trail

The Prairie View Trail begins at the entrance to Moore Creek Preserve on Highway 1. The trail follows cow paths which are still used by the cattle on the property. The footing is very uneven and in some places the paths are overgrown and difficult to follow. However, the views of the meadow and the ocean are quite beautiful. Proceed .7 miles past the Moore Creek Trail on your right. Continue straight ahead up the incline to the Terrace Loop Trail signpost. Turn right and follow the Terrace Loop Trail .4 miles as it curves up and back to the Prairie View Trail. The Terrace Loop trail is also a grassy overgrown cow path. At the top you will reach the intersection of the Terrace Loop and Prairie View Trails where you could turn right to reach the Vernal Ridge Trail. However, at the time of this writing the Vernal Ridge Trail was still under development, and it is difficult to find the actual footpath once you leave the straight trail that borders the property boundary fence. We recommend you turn left at the intersection and rejoin the Prairie View Trail to complete the loop. This loop is entirely visible as it travels through open meadow.

Moore Creek Trail

Begin on the Prairie View Trail, which ascends from Highway 1 through a wide open meadow. At .7 miles turn right on the Moore Creek Trail. This newly renovated trail follows rolling terrain, crosses Moore Creek on a year-round bridge and climbs up from the creek to Meder Street. While the Prairie View Trail is little more than a cow path, the Moore Creek Trail is a well defined single-track trail with good footing. It is moderately strenuous as it climbs through the meadows and woods of the preserve. At Meder Street, reverse your direction back to Highway 1.

Distance and Difficulty

**Prairie View/
Terrace Loop Trail**
2.4 miles with one hill.

Moore Creek Trail
2.6 miles round trip with one moderate hill.

Safety

Beware of rutted, narrow trails which are not well used and quite isolated.

Other Things You Should Know

The entrance to the Moore Creek Preserve is on Highway 1 just as it leaves Santa Cruz heading north. You can park across the highway on Schaffer Road. There is no water or restroom available.

For more information and updates about the status of trails, call the City of Santa Cruz Parks and Recreation Department or go to their website at www. santacruzparksandrec.com.

MOORE CREEK PRESERVE

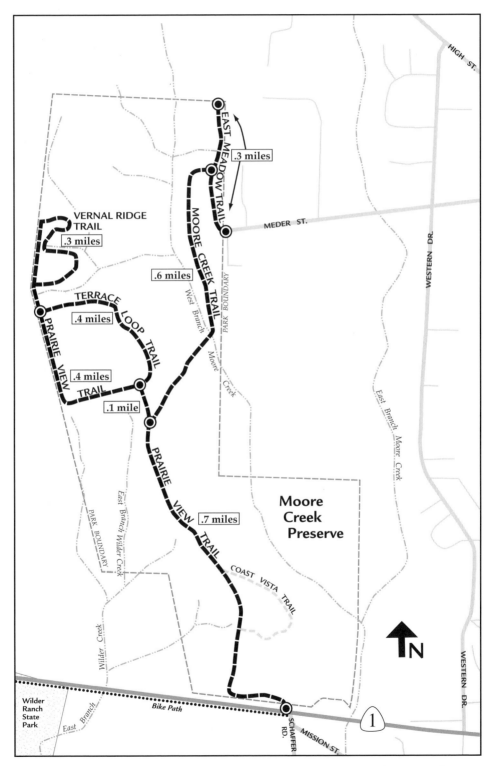

UCSC CAMPUS NATURAL RESERVE

The fire roads winding through the UCSC Campus Natural Reserve offer a great place for moderately strenuous runs or walks through a beautiful and diverse mountain landscape. UCSC faculty member Ken Norris founded the reserve in 1988 in order to protect intact natural communities for study. He called it an "outdoor laboratory" and "a classroom without walls." These 400 acres showcase a diverse range of environments, including redwoods, prairies, chaparral, and mountain springs.

Route and Features
Chinquapin Road

Chinquapin Road is the longest of the natural reserve trails. Its trailhead can be reached from the parking lot behind the firehouse (past Crown College on the paved road also called Chinquapin). After a short hill, Chinquapin Road trail is mostly flat with a slow incline all the way to the twin gates at Empire Grade Road. At the twin gates, Chinquapin crosses Empire Grade Road and continues into Wilder Ranch State Park. (See the Long Meadow Trail description in the Wilder Ranch section on page 43.)

Alternative Loops

Intersecting Chinquapin Road are Fuel Break Road, Red Hill Road, and West Road. You can use any of these roads to vary your route. West Road and Red Hill Road are moderately steep but short climbs from the campus up to Fuel Break Road. After intersecting Fuel Break Road, they both flatten out and continue to Chinquapin Road. You can also begin your run from the trail head for West Road, which is located behind the North Remote parking lot at the end of Heller Drive. The trails and intersections within the reserve are well marked. (Some of the campus mileage indicators don't agree with our figures. Check our map for recently measured distances.)

While the UCSC Campus Natural Reserve permits use of these trails, walkers and runners are requested to be respectful of the natural environment and the ongoing research which is conducted here. Visitors must stay on the trails and move carefully through this area.

Distance and Difficulty

Chinquapin Road
A moderate 4.4-mile round trip with mild incline.

Alternative Loops
1-to 2-mile loops with some short climbs.

Safety

The trails are well used by pedestrians, runners and cyclists. However, the trails are remote and caution is required. Mountain lions have been sighted in this area. Read the signs for mountain lion safety tips. Parts of these trails are quite exposed and hot in the summer. We recommend carrying water for long excursions.

Other Things You Should Know

Metered parking on the campus is usually available on weekends and when school is not in session. Parking on campus while classes are in session is difficult. Some lots allow parking without permits on weekends. There are no restrooms or water on these trails.

UCSC CAMPUS NATURAL RESERVE

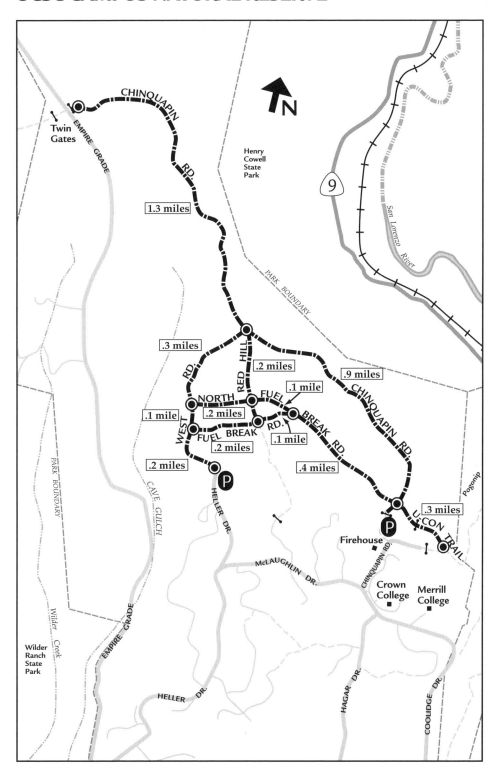

NATURAL BRIDGES STATE BEACH AND ANTONELLI POND

The trails of Natural Bridges State Beach are perfect for a short, quiet run or walk through forest, meadow, marsh, and beach. Natural Bridges State Beach is named after the rock arches that used to stand in the water near the entrance. Today only one of the three rock arches for which this park was named still stands. The outer arch fell in the early 1900's and the inner arch collapsed during a storm in 1980. Natural Bridges is also famous as a fall and winter home for Monarch butterflies.

North of Natural Bridges State Beach is Antonelli Pond, created by the damming of Moore Creek in 1909. It was originally used as a millpond by the San Vicente Lumber Company and then later used by the Antonelli Brothers for their begonia gardens. Today it is publicly owned and you can occasionally see a small rowboat or canoe on its waters or a fisherman hoping for a catch.

Route and Features

If you begin at the main park entrance, run down the hill. Look carefully to your right for the entrance to the nature trail. Proceed along the trail a few hundred yards to a "T" intersection. Turn right heading north along the trail. (If you go left, you'll go down a rocky trail past a small pond to a boardwalk and the monarch butterfly observation area.) Traverse a well-worn nature path through the meadow and under the trees. Cross the service road and proceed on the dirt road (now called the Moore Creek Trail), where you will pass numbered signposts. At .5 miles veer left and continue along the nature trail loop. At this point you can see a lovely view of the remaining arch. You will cross several boardwalks laid across the marsh and emerge onto the beach. During high winter tides you may need to return the way you came. Most of the year, however, you can head left onto the beach and across the sand to the restrooms. (There is often a seasonal lagoon requiring you to climb across the rocks for a few yards to get back onto the beach.) After you get to the restrooms, go up the path to the road and turn right to return to the park entrance.

To include Antonelli Pond, veer right at another "T", this one on the Moore Creek Trail. Cross Delaware Avenue. Antonelli Pond will be in front of you, though it is hidden from view. Run 50 yards to your left along Delaware to find the entrance to the dirt trail. The trail runs alongside the pond for .3 miles and ends at the railroad trestle. Because the trestle is in severe disrepair, we recommend that you turn back to return to Natural Bridges rather than try to cross to the other side. The east side of Antonelli Pond also has a trail running .3 miles. It runs along the side of the old Lipton plant and doesn't afford much of a view of the pond.

Distance and Difficulty

This run is a flat, easy 1.3-mile loop for runners and walkers of all levels. Most of the run is along dirt trails, with short stretches on a boardwalk and along the beach. The Antonelli Pond trail's quick side trip adds .8 miles to your run.

Safety

The Natural Bridges nature trail is well marked and well worn. It is fairly quiet except during monarch season when visitors are abundant. Antonelli Pond is hidden from the road and occasionally used by dog walkers and others.

Other Things You Should Know

There is on-street parking available near the main entrance along Swanton Boulevard and at the rear entrance on Delaware Avenue. You can also pay the state park admission fee and park in the lot at the picnic and beach area. Restrooms and drinking fountains are located off the parking lot, at the visitor center, and at the northeast side of the beach.

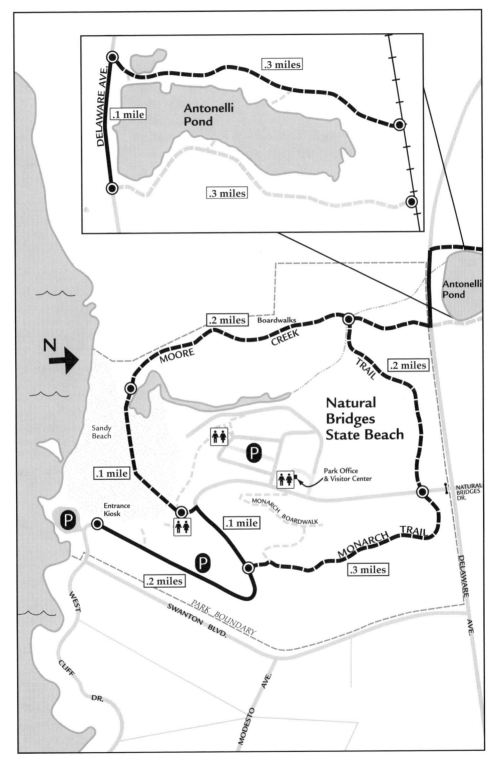

HENRY COWELL REDWOODS STATE PARK: HIGHWAY 9 ENTRANCE

From the easy and well used Redwood Loop, to the wild, rugged, and isolated climbs of the Rincon Fire Road, Henry Cowell State Park offers visitors a variety of choices. The trails lead you through stands of ancient redwoods and alongside a rushing San Lorenzo River. Henry Cowell State Park was created in 1954 by combining land donated by S.H. Cowell with land from the former Santa Cruz County Big Trees Park. The park is named in honor of Henry Cowell, the father of S.H. Cowell. Henry Cowell, a successful Santa Cruz businessman, came from Massachusetts during the Gold Rush and began a business supplying miners. After the Gold Rush he started a limestone business, operating several quarries in Santa Cruz and Felton. The kilns and the barrel mill site can still be seen in the Fall Creek section of the park.

Routes and Features.

Redwood Grove Loop Trail

Redwood Grove Loop Trail is a .8-mile circle which brings you past many of the largest redwood trees in the park. It is flat and soft underfoot. It can be crowded with tourists, especially in the summer and on weekends, which makes running difficult. The loop is less crowded in early mornings and in the winter.

River Trail Loop

The River Trail can be accessed from behind the gift shop. Follow the road to your left. Go past the first trail sign for the River Trail and proceed to your next right on the paved road. Here you will find a trail kiosk detailing distances, trails and directions. The trail begins as a gentle, flat path along the San Lorenzo River. It is also open to equestrian use and is soft and wide as you might expect a bridal path to be. It crosses Pipeline Road as it passes under the train trestle and continues along the river. At the Eagle Creek Trail intersection, the River Trail turns right over a small bridge, parallels the small creek and climbs moderately through the redwoods towards the ridge. The San Lorenzo River can be heard and, at times, glimpsed far below. While this section of the trail climbs, it is not too steep. The footing is good and can be managed by most well-conditioned runners.

The River Trail ends at Rincon Fire Road. Turn left, for a long, gradual downhill run on a soft dirt trail. At the intersection with Pipeline Road turn left. Look carefully for the trail marker for Eagle Creek Trail on your left. It is somewhat difficult to see as it is set back from the road. (You will first see another sign for the Eagle Creek Trail on your right but you want to take the trail to your left.) After .1 mile you intersect with the River Trail. Retrace your steps back to the gift shop. You can

(continued on page 53)

Distance and Difficulty

Redwood Grove Loop Trail
An easy, flat .8-mile loop on a wide, packed dirt trail.

River Trail Loop
An easy-to-moderate 2.5-mile loop from the nature center. The first .6 miles is flat and then the trail climbs for .5 miles. The return is .4 miles down and then flat for 1 mile.

Eagle Creek Loop
From the Nature Center a 4.6-mile moderate-to-strenuous loop of gradual-to-moderate uphill and gradual-to-steep downhill on dirt trails with good footing. There is a half-mile section of deep sand.

HENRY COWELL REDWOODS STATE PARK: HIGHWAY 9 ENTRANCE

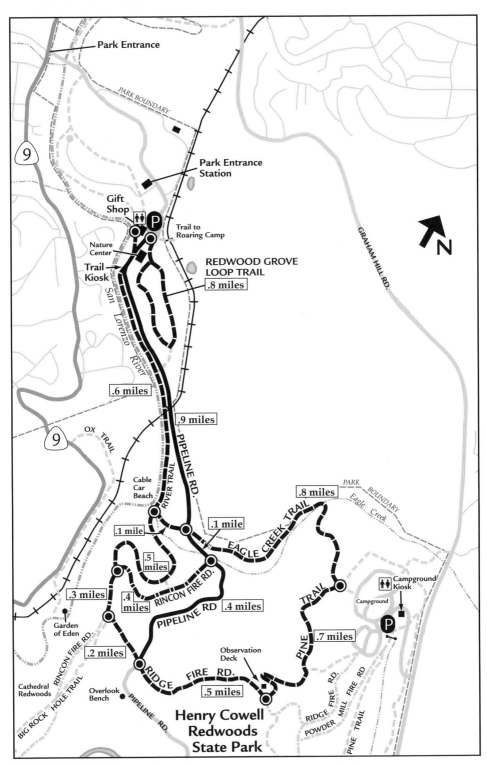

Park Entrance

PARK BOUNDARY

9

Park Entrance
Station

Gift
Shop

P

Trail to
Roaring Camp

Nature
Center

REDWOOD GROVE
LOOP TRAIL

Trail
Kiosk

.8 miles

San Lorenzo River

GRAHAM HILL RD.

N

.6 miles

9

OX TRAIL

.9 miles

PIPELINE RD.

Cable
Car
Beach

RIVER TRAIL

PARK BOUNDARY

Eagle Creek

.8 miles

EAGLE CREEK TRAIL

.1 mile

.1 mile

.5
miles

Campground
Kiosk

PINE TRAIL

Campground

.3 miles

.4
miles

RINCON FIRE RD.

PIPELINE RD

.4 miles

P

Garden
of Eden

RINCON FIRE RD.

.2 miles

Observation
Deck

.7 miles

PINE

RIDGE FIRE RD.

Cathedral
Redwoods

BIG ROCK HOLE TRAIL

Overlook
Bench

PIPELINE RD.

RIDGE FIRE RD.

.5 miles

POWDER MILL FIRE RD

RIDGE FIRE RD.

PINE TRAIL

Henry Cowell
Redwoods
State Park

Above: Crossing Eagle Creek along the River Trail.

Below: 2000-year-old redwood cross section at the entrance to the Redwood Grove Loop Trail.

also continue on the Pipeline Road back to the gift shop rather than returning to the River Trail.

Eagle Creek Loop

Access the River Trail as above. Follow the trail .6 miles to the Eagle Creek Trail. At .1 mile Eagle Creek Trail crosses Pipeline Road and then climbs .8 miles to the campground. This is a single-track trail running alongside the creek. There is good footing and the climb ranges from moderate to steep. At the top of the hill the trail becomes very sandy and exposed. You have moved out of the redwoods and into the oak and madrone forest. Be sure to stay in the center of the trail as there is plenty of poison oak along the side. At the trail intersection turn right onto Pine Trail. There is a sign to direct you. Follow the sandy Pine Trail .7 miles to the observation deck and Ridge Fire Road trail. There are two water fountains at the base of the deck. One is for horses. You'll have a great view of the Monterey Bay and Santa Cruz Beach Boardwalk from the top of the observation deck. Continue around the observation deck to Ridge Fire Road trail. Read the markers carefully as several trails intersect here. Although a multi-use fire road, the trail is very narrow here. It continues to be sandy and exposed and you even pass through a small sand canyon.

The trail returns to the redwood forest and is mostly downhill from here. At .5 miles Ridge Fire Road intersects with Pipeline Road. If you turn right, you will return 1.4 miles to the gift shop by way of Pipeline Road, which is paved and descends steeply. Alternatively, you can continue across Pipeline Road on Ridge Fire Road .2 miles to Rincon Fire Road. Turn right. Rincon Fire Road will bring you gradually .7 miles down to Pipeline Road on good soft footing. Turn left and continue 1 mile to the gift shop on Pipeline Road or look for the sign for Eagle Creek Trail a few yards to your left. It can be difficult to spot. Continue .1 mile on Eagle Creek Trail to River Trail and then retrace your steps .6 miles to the gift shop.

Safety

The Redwood Grove Loop Trail is fully accessible, with excellent footing. It is well used, especially on weekends and during the summer tourist season. The River Trail also receives a lot of use up to the intersection with Eagle Creek Trail, as does Pipeline Road. The Eagle Creek Loop receives a lot of use, especially from campers, except when the campground is closed December through February. The rest of the trails in the park are quite isolated. Many involve climbs and uneven footing. While quite placid in the summer, the San Lorenzo River can run fast and deep in the winter.

Other Things You Should Know

There are restrooms and water at the campground, picnic area and gift shop.

The state park has a large parking area. Fees are collected.

HENRY COWELL REDWOODS STATE PARK: GRAHAM HILL ENTRANCE

The Graham Hill Trail entrance can be found on Graham Hill Road north of Sims Road just past the Graham Hill Mini Market. There is a short, almost hidden frontage road here with parking for a limited number of cars. If you are heading north on Graham Hill, look for the turnout on the left just past the intersection of Graham Hill Road and Tree Top Drive.

Routes and Features

Graham Hill Trail Loop

From Graham Hill Road on the south side of the park perimeter, a loop can be made using Graham Hill Trail, Pine Trail, Powder Mill Fire Road and Powder Mill Trail. The loop begins at the intersection of the Pipeline Road, Powder Mill Trail, and Graham Hill Trail at the south boundary of the park on Graham Hill Road. The trailhead is at the north end of the frontage road parking area. Graham Hill Trail parallels Graham Hill Road. The loop trail is flat through mixed wood forest. While you are in the woods, you are only 100 yards or so from the road and the noise of the traffic is evident. Graham Hill Trail ends near the park entrance station. There is a left turn marked here for the Pine Trail. Pine Trail travels into the park and away from the road. At .8 miles it intersects with the unpaved Powder Mill Fire Road. Turn left on Powder Mill Fire Road heading to Powder Mill Trail. The fire road is packed sand and dirt and can be quite mucky in the winter. After traveling .5 miles down the road, you'll come to the intersection of Powder Mill Fire Road and Powder Mill Trail. Turn left onto the trail, which dips steeply down the ravine to Powder Mill Creek. This creek is easy to cross except after winter storms. Continue up the trail back to Graham Hill Trail to complete the loop.

Pine Trail Loop

Another trail accessed from the south side of the park is the Pine Trail. It loops around the campground from Graham Hill Trail. The trail is quite sandy for most of its length and travels through redwood forests, exposed manzanita and other low brush. Follow Graham Hill Trail (as described above) to the entrance to Pine Trail near the park entrance station. Turning left off of Graham Hill Trail, take Pine Trail and continue on it across Powder Mill Fire Road until you reach the observation deck. Here you can get a great view of the San Lorenzo River Valley to the ocean. There is also a water fountain. Continue on the Pine Trail as it loops around the campground back to Graham Hill Trail. Take the Graham Hill Trail back to the parking area.

Distance and Difficulty

Graham Hill Trail Loop

An easy-to-moderate 3.6-mile loop of single-track trail and unpaved road through the woods.

Pine Trail Loop

An easy-to-moderate 5.6-mile loop which combines Pine Trail and Graham Hill Trail. A half-mile section of the Pine Trail is very sandy.

Safety

The trails are quite isolated and not well used, especially November to February when the campground is closed. Horses share the road.

Other Things You Should Know

There are restrooms and water at the campground.

HENRY COWELL REDWOODS STATE PARK: GRAHAM HILL ENTRANCE

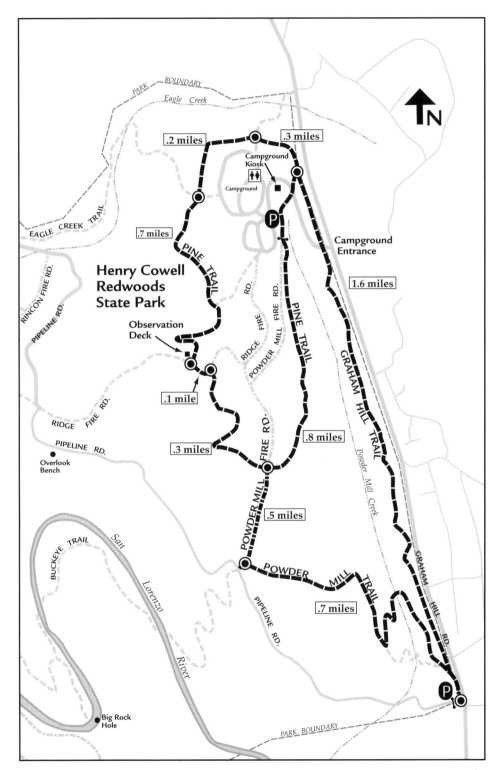

FALL CREEK

The 2,390 acres of Fall Creek offer wonderfully scenic and rugged trails. Fall Creek, the northern unit of Henry Cowell State Park, features a year-round rushing creek and is the former site of a great limestone quarry. The lime kiln area within the park contains large abandoned kilns used to remove lime from limestone. At the Barrel Mill Site, barrels for packing the lime were made with lumber from the surrounding redwood trees. Fall Creek is an undeveloped park with no facilities of any kind.

Routes and Features

Trail to Lime Kilns

From the Fall Creek parking area descend gradually on the single-track Bennett Trail .2 miles through the forest to the Fall Creek Trail, which travels along Fall Creek. The trail is wide and flat in most places. The creek is especially beautiful as it runs toward the San Lorenzo River. At the trail intersection turn left on the Lime Kiln Trail to the lime kilns site. This trail runs along the south fork of Fall Creek, which has a small water flow. The trail is rocky and you will climb several rocky steps on the way to the lime kilns.

Trail to Barrel Mill Site

The .2 mile Bennett Trail leads from the parking lot to the Fall Creek Trail. Turn left on the Fall Creek Trail. After the intersection with the Lime Kiln Trail, continue along the Fall Creek Trail as it becomes a single-track trail. You will be following the trail alongside Fall Creek. This flat section of the trail involves several stream crossings, which are easy in summer when the seasonal bridges are in place (April–October). When the creek runs at fuller volume during the winter rains, it may be impossible to cross. You can sometimes cross on fallen logs and boulders, though you may get your feet wet. At 2.6 miles you will come to the Barrel Mill Site. The remnants of the mill machinery are well preserved and you can easily explore the site. Retrace your steps to return to the parking lot.

Big Ben Trail Loop

Follow the trail description for the Barrel Mill Site above. After passing the Barrel Mill Site, continue on the Fall Creek Trail for .6 miles and cross the creek. The trail, now called Big Ben Trail, climbs steeply up the side of Ben Lomond Mountain through drier forest to the ridge. This is a difficult climb and the trail seems a lot longer than the trail markers indicate. Plan on doubling the time you estimate it will take you to complete this loop if you are walking, and allow one-and-a-half times as much if you are running. The trail, which turns into Lost Empire Trail 1.4 miles from Fall Creek Trail, travels along the ridge before beginning its descent back to Fall Creek Trail. At this intersection, you can return directly to the parking area via the Fall Creek Trail or you can add .3 miles more by looping through the lime kiln site by way of the Cape Horn Trail.

Distance and Difficulty

Trail to Lime Kilns
A 2.4-mile easy-to-moderate out-and-back trail used by school groups, hikers and runners.

Trail to Barrel Mill Site
A 5.2-mile, mostly flat, easy-to-moderate out and back trail.

Big Ben Trail Loop
A steep, strenuous 8.1-mile loop that climbs up the side of Ben Lomond Mountain.

Safety

The Fall Creek trails are not well used beyond the lime kilns.

The creek crossings can be difficult and slippery when the seasonal bridges are not in place.

Other Things You Should Know

Fall Creek has a small free parking area located on Felton Empire Road .6 miles past the Felton Village and Highway 9 intersection. Watch carefully for the entrance on the right, past the Felton Cemetery. It is difficult to spot the sign indicating the turn into the parking lot. Fall Creek has no restrooms, outhouses or water fountains.

FALL CREEK

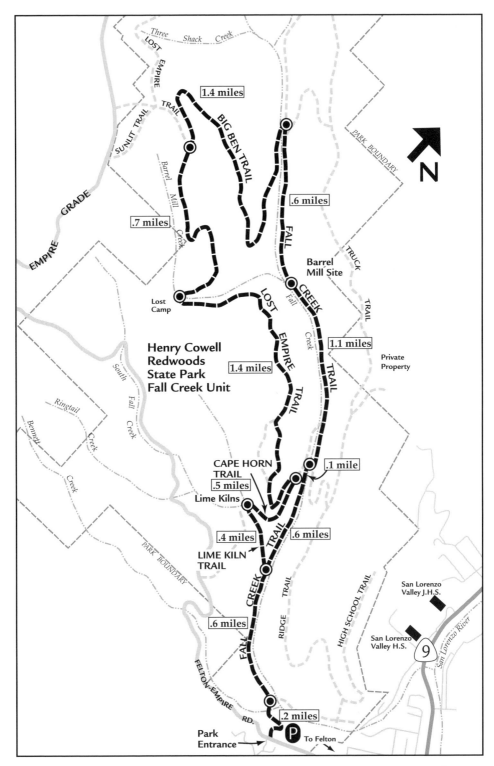

UPPER POGONIP:
SPRING STREET ENTRANCE

Pogonip offers all the features of good trail running and walking. You will find wide, flat fire roads, single-track trails which vary from mild to rugged, as well as shade, sun, forest and meadows. Beginners to advanced runners can enjoy running here. Owned by the City of Santa Cruz, Pogonip was once part of the extensive Henry Cowell Ranch holdings. It is also the former home of the Pogonip Country Club and prior to that the Santa Cruz Golf and Country Club. The Pogonip Country Club offered polo, horseback riding swimming and tennis. The clubhouse still stands and there is talk of renovating it for public use. Currently horses can be seen grazing in the meadow. The origin of the name is a bit of a mystery. It may derive from a Shoshone Indian term describing a dense winter fog. Considering the dense fog that often enshrouds Santa Cruz, this seems to be an appropriate name.

Route and Features
Spring and Rincon Trail
At the walk-in entrance off Spring Street, turn right onto the Spring Trail. The beginning of the trail is rutted with uneven footing. After the first .3 miles of open meadow the trail is shaded and the footing is good, with one short muddy section in winter. Spring Trail is a wide flat fire road which intersects the Rincon Trail at 1.6 miles. Continue straight ahead on the Rincon Trail for .1 mile to the locked gate. We recommend you turn around here. Beyond this point, Rincon Trail drops steeply .2 miles down to Highway 9.

Lime Kiln Trail and Spring Box Trail Loop
A nice variation on the out-and-back Spring and Rincon Trail is to take the Lime Kiln and Spring Box Trails. These trails form a short loop back down to Spring Trail. Begin your run on Spring Trail as described above. At 1.6 miles, just past the intersection of the Rincon and Spring Trails you will see the Lime Kiln Trail on your left. This trail is a short but steep climb through forest on a single-track trail. It travels .3 miles to the top of the abandoned lime kilns. The kilns are remnants of the days when lime was manufactured on the ranch which once stood here. The lime works were bought by Henry Cowell, whose family later donated land to the University of California. The lime kilns were active from 1849 until 1911. The Lime Kiln Trail turns sharply to the left here and joins the Rincon Trail. Turn right on the Rincon Trail, run past the lime kilns now fully visible to you, and look for the Spring Box Trail about 50 yards or so on your left. The single-track Spring Box Trail travels .3 miles past a small stream, large redwood trees, and a meadow back down to the Spring Trail.

Distance and Difficulty

Spring and Rincon Trail
A flat out-and-back 3.4-mile round trip unpaved fire road.

Lime Kiln and Spring Box Trail Loop
A 3.2-mile flat loop with one moderate hill.

Lookout Trail Loop
A moderate-to-strenuous 3.1-mile loop with one steep .3-mile climb.

Safety

While the Spring Trail gets a lot of use by runners and walkers, the other trails are not well used. This is also mountain lion country. Read the signs so you are aware of what to do in case you encounter a mountain lion.

(continued on page 61)

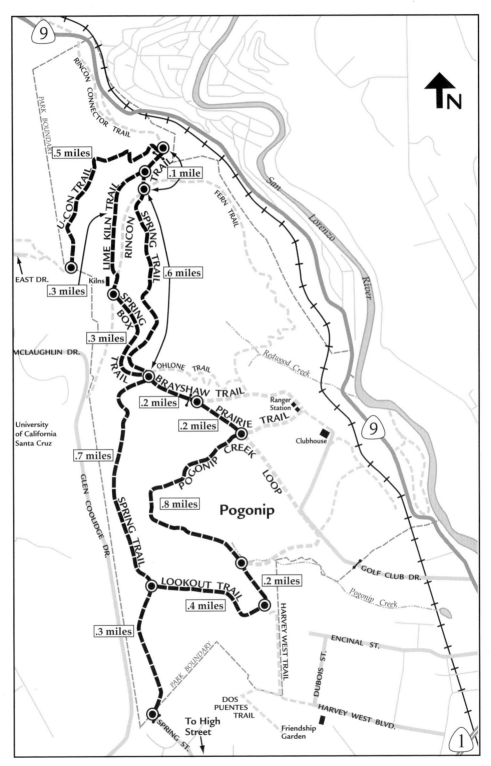

Above: The view from Upper Pogonip.

Below: Maggie on the Spring Trail.

Lookout Trail Loop

Begin on the Spring Trail. At .3 miles turn right onto the Lookout Trail. This .4-mile trail begins flat and then turns steeply downhill, bringing you to the lower Pogonip. At the intersection with the Pogonip Creek and Harvey West Trails, turn left. Turn left again at the next signpost for the Pogonip Creek Loop. The Pogonip Creek Loop offers forest and meadow trail running and comes within sight of the old clubhouse. At the intersection with the Prairie Trail, turn left and head up the hill. At the gate, turn left into a short, very steep and rocky section of the Brayshaw Trail. Watch your footing. At the Spring Trail turn left to complete the loop.

. . . .

There is a new connector trail (called the U-Con Trail) created to allow bicycle access between Henry Cowell State Park, the UCSC Campus Natural Reserve, and Wilder Ranch. A cyclist or well-conditioned runner can now make a complete trek all the way from Henry Cowell to Highway 1. The U-Con Trail is a very steep, half-mile climb and you must give right of way to cyclists, as this is their only access through Pogonip.

While we have separately described the upper and lower Pogonip, there is no natural boundary between them. All trails are accessible from both the Spring Street and Harvey West Park (Dos Puentes Trail) entrances. Lower trails are those that descend toward Highway 9, while the upper trails tend to run up the ridge toward UCSC. The exception is Lookout Trail, which connects the ridge near UCSC with the lower sections of the park. Lookout Trail is easily reached from either entrance.

Other Things You Should Know

There are no restrooms or water in Pogonip. All the trails are well marked with park signs and mileage.

To reach the Spring Street entrance to Pogonip, turn north off High Street onto Spring Street. Spring Street ends at the park entrance. There is limited on-street parking in this residential neighborhood.

LOWER POGONIP:
HARVEY WEST PARK ENTRANCE

The new Dos Puentes Trail, created in 2002, gives easy access to Pogonip from Harvey West Park, where there is plenty of on- and off-street parking available. The trail begins next to the Friendship Garden behind the swimming pool. Walk to the end of Harvey West Boulevard and look for the trailhead in front of you on the park side of the fence. The trail is well marked.

Routes and Features

Pogonip Creek Trail Loop

The Pogonip Creek Trail is a beautiful route through redwoods, along a creek, and across the meadow of the old Pogonip Club. Begin on Dos Puentes Trail at the far northwest corner of Harvey West Park. At the first trail intersection, turn sharply right onto Harvey West Trail. Follow the trail around the side of the hill for .5 miles. After a steep climb in which you will see a view of Santa Cruz and the buildings of the Harvey West Business Park to your right, you will come to level ground where Harvey West Trail merges with Lookout Trail. Take a short jog to your right and immediately left on the Lookout Trail. Do not continue straight ahead. (Watch carefully for this u-shaped turnoff. If you start to climb very steeply you have missed the turn off.) Follow the lower part of Lookout Trail .2 miles to Pogonip Creek Trail. At the Pogonip Creek Trail marker, you will have the choice of following this circular loop in either direction. We suggest turning to your left so that much of the uphill will be in the shade. You will run through the redwoods, uphill across a hidden meadow, back into the redwoods, and then out into the large meadow. At the intersection with the Prairie Trail, turn right to stay on the Pogonip Creek Trail downhill through the meadow, back into the redwoods and back to the beginning of the loop.

Fern Trail Loop

The Fern Trail is a strenuous and deceiving .8-mile trail. It is steep, with many switchbacks as it descends the side of the canyon towards Highway 9. The footing is uneven, and you should plan on taking twice as long as you would think to complete this section of the loop. Although difficult, the trail is the most beautiful in the park. Follow the directions above for the Pogonip Creek Trail, but at the intersection with Prairie Trail cross the meadow and continue straight ahead on Prairie Trail to the small ranger stand. Turn left on Brayshaw Trail for .2 miles and then right on Fern Trail. After a short, flat part of the trail, you will begin to descend to the Redwood Creek crossing. You will then begin a continuous ascent. The trail opens out into meadow as it climbs uphill. At the top of the trail turn left onto the Spring Trail fire road and go .6 miles to Brayshaw Trail. Brayshaw Trail runs steeply downhill on a rocky fire road. When you come to the gate on your right, go through it onto Prairie Trail and run through the meadow back to Pogonip Creek Trail. Continue downhill and into the redwoods for your return.

Distance and Difficulty

Pogonip Creek Trail Loop
A moderately hilly 2.8-mile loop

Fern Trail Loop
A strenuous 4.6-mile loop

Safety

The lower trails are not well used. Caution is needed on the trails that cross the meadow, as the footing can be quite uneven. This is also mountain lion country. Read the signs so you are aware of what to do in case you encounter a mountain lion. There are often horses grazing in the meadow and you should keep a suitable distance.

Other Things You Should Know

Parking is available at the Harvey West Park entrance. There are no restrooms or water in Pogonip. The only restrooms and water are at the Harvey West swimming pool. All the trails are well marked with park signs and mileage.

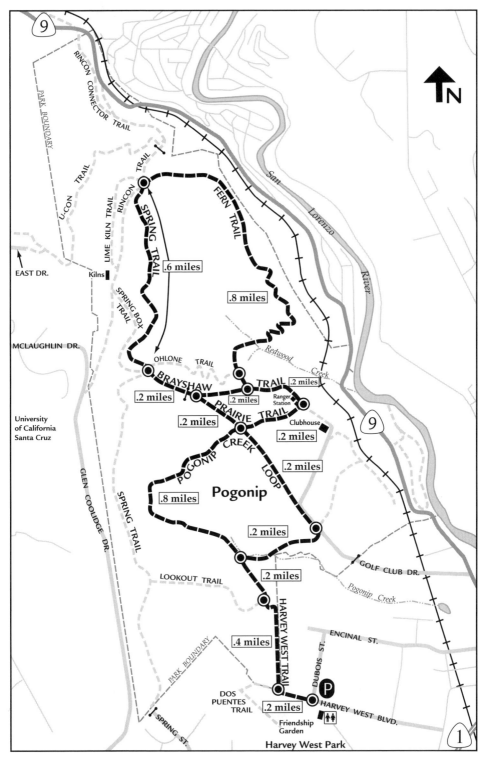

DELAVEAGA PARK

Conveniently located on the east side of Santa Cruz, DeLaveaga Park offers single-track and dirt road trail running. Most of the trails are shaded and wooded. The park stands on the grounds of the former country estate of José Vincent de Laveaga. He developed this estate in the 1880's and donated the land to the public on his death in 1894. His estate had a home for the deaf and at one time housed a zoo. The park now consists of softball fields, large picnic areas, a playground, a golf course, a disc golf course, an archery range and a pistol shooting range.

Route and Features

Entrance to the running trails is from the lower park area. This area is where the softball fields, picnic area and playgrounds can be found. To find the entrance to the trails, go up the steps alongside the restrooms next to the BBQ area. Turn right on the trail and climb up to the dirt road. From here you have several choices.

Lower Loop

When you reach the intersection of the trail from the picnic area and the dirt road, turn right. Look for the trailhead on your left before you reach the gate. There is no trail marker and it is easy to miss. If you reach the park entrance, you have gone too far. This lower loop trail meanders through the woods close to the road. It is a gentle trail for all ability levels. Beware of the large amount of poison oak on this very narrow trail. At .6 miles turn left at the fork, make the hairpin turn, and continue on the single-track trail through the woods to Sand Pit Road. Turn left on the fire road. In 100 yards you will be back at the start.

Top of the World Trail

Make a hairpin left turn just before the trail from the BBQ area meets the dirt road and continue on the single-track trail. You need to run cautiously here as there are many roots and uneven surfaces and the trail is quite narrow. As the trail climbs steadily uphill, you will pass through several open spaces with views across the Branciforte Creek Valley. After a long stretch of shade, at 1.5 miles, the trail flattens out in a small open space. The trail continues on your right up a rocky step-like path. The trail ends at the Corona Lookout, locally known as The Top of the World, where there is a beautiful view of the Monterey Bay.

Sand Pit Road

Sand Pit Road is a gently climbing, well used fire road which begins at the pull-out on Branciforte Drive and ends at the golf course. Many dog walkers and mountain bikers share this road with runners. You can only travel out and back as you are not allowed to cross the golf course fairways. You can also access the lower loop and Top of the World Trail from this fire road.

Distance and Difficulty

The trails are not named at DeLaveaga Park. Locals distinguish them as the lower trails between Branciforte Drive and the fire road and the Top of the World Trail, which begins behind the restrooms near the large picnic and BBQ area.

Lower Loop
A 1.3-mile loop of easy, relatively flat trail running

Top of the World Trail
A 3-mile moderately strenuous out-and-back single-track trail with many tree roots and an uneven surface.

Sand Pit Road
A 2-mile round trip on a wide dirt road with a moderate grade.

Safety

Be aware of cyclists and uneven terrain on these trails. They are well used, especially on weekends. There is a lot of poison oak along the lower trails.

Other Things You Should Know

Parking is free at the picnic areas. Restrooms and water fountains are available at the entrance to the trails.

DELAVEAGA PARK

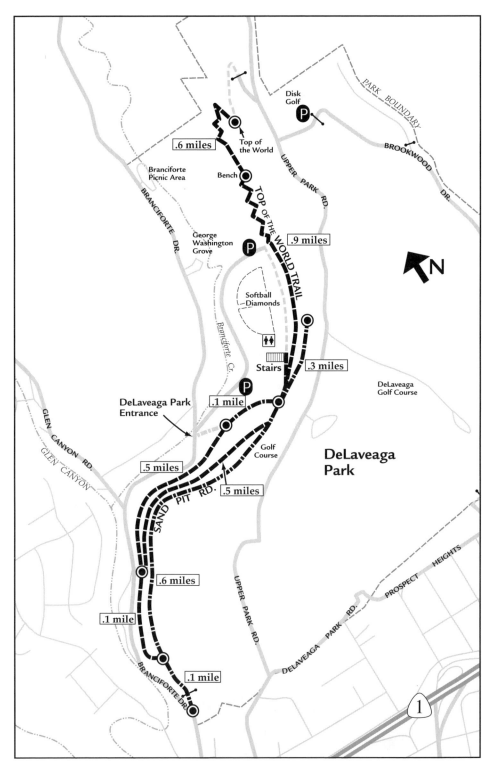

Disk Golf

PARK BOUNDARY

BROOKWOOD DR.

UPPER PARK RD.

.6 miles

Top of the World

Branciforte Picnic Area

Bench

TOP OF THE WORLD TRAIL

.9 miles

George Washington Grove

N

Softball Diamonds

Branciforte Cr.

Stairs

.3 miles

DeLaveaga Golf Course

.1 mile

DeLaveaga Park Entrance

.5 miles

Golf Course

DeLaveaga Park

GLEN CANYON RD.

GLEN CANYON

SAND PIT RD.

.5 miles

.6 miles

UPPER PARK RD.

PROSPECT HEIGHTS

.1 mile

BRANCIFORTE DR.

DELAVEAGA PARK RD.

.1 mile

BRANCIFORTE DR.

1

SCHWAN LAKE PARK

This hidden park is a perfect place for a short, quiet run. Schwan Lake Park is part of Twin Lakes State Beach and is in the area behind Schwan Lake. (The lake is often referred to as Schwan Lagoon.) It is home to many birds and a flock of geese. Schwan Lake is one of the two lakes which give the area the name of Twin Lakes. The other is Woods Lake (aka Woods Lagoon), which was dredged to create the Santa Cruz Harbor.

Route and Features

The entrance to the park is at the back of the Simpkins Family Swim Center parking lot. A kiosk and signpost mark the entrance to the trail. The main trail is a narrow dirt road which winds through woods and meadow and along the lagoon.

The dirt road is made up of two loops shaped like a backwards B. The loop nearest the parking lot passes by low shrubs and alongside a stand of trees. The furthest loop winds through woods and meadow and alongside the lagoon. The lagoon is often covered with lily pads, and ducks and frogs are abundant. The trail is shaded by trees for half its length and travels through open meadow for its other half. It would be difficult to get lost here – you can run the loops in any direction and in any combination that you like and you will always end up back on the straight trail you started on. The few side single-track trails that you pass all cross the meadow back to the dirt road.

Distance and Difficulty

A mostly flat, 1.1-mile run for all levels of runners. There is one very short steep down and up in the center of the park.

Safety

As with all parks that are relatively isolated and uncrowded, we recommend staying on the main trails and not running alone.

Other Things You Should Know

To reach the entrance to Schwan Lake Park, go to the end of the parking lot at the Simpkins Family Swim Center. The driveway to the swim center is located on the west side of 17th Avenue between Brommer and East Cliff, right next to the railroad tracks. When the Swim Center is closed, you can also access the trails by parking on El Dorado Street, just north of Brommer and 17th, and walking across the railroad tracks.

There is plenty of parking in the swim center parking lot. When the center is open, there is a restroom and water – and in fact you might want to combine your run with a trip to the pool. The swim center hours vary with the season, so be sure to call ahead.

SCHWAN LAKE PARK

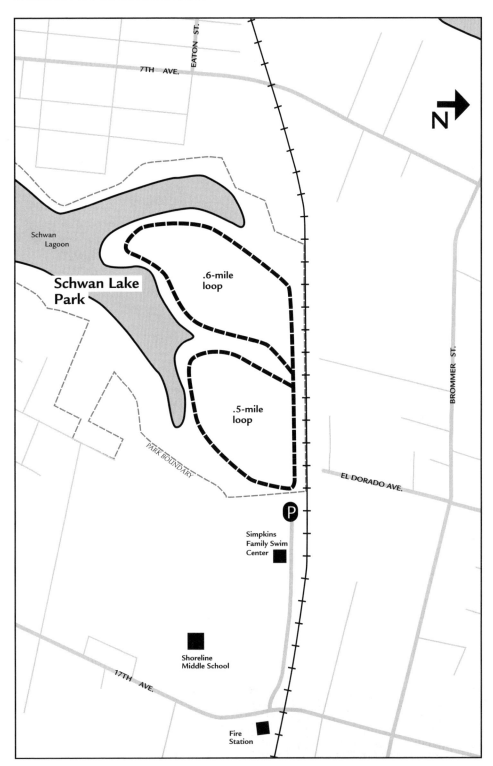

ANNA JEAN CUMMINGS PARK

This new park in Soquel is a great alternative to street running. It has a soft, wide, measured flat path as well as dirt trails. There is a playground for children and soccer and softball fields. The park is named for Anna Jean Cummings, founder of the Santa Cruz Land Trust and member of the Save Soquel group that helped secure this former O'Neill Dairy Ranch property as public recreational and open space.

Route and Features

Jogging and Walking Path

The jogging path which encircles the soccer and softball fields is a great alternative to street and track running. The majority of the path is packed dirt, which is easy on the legs, with the soft surface cushioning the type of shock that you might get on asphalt. You can easily keep track of your mileage, and you can run with friends or family. Since you have a view of the entire path from every vantage point, you can keep track of children who may not be running at the same speed as you. Some experienced runners like to do their interval or speed running here since the flat, smooth surface allows for very consistent running. The path is .5 miles long. The path circling just the softball field is .35 miles long. The path circling just the soccer field is .3 miles long.

Killer Hill Trail

This trail above the Soquel High School baseball field is an old trail which is now more easily accessible since the completion of the county park. To access this trail, go to the end of the Anna Jean Cummings parking lot. Directly in front of you is what is known as "Killer Hill." The name gives you some indication of the steepness of the climb. It is, however, very short. You are rewarded with a 360° view of the Monterey Bay and the Soquel Hills. At the top of "Killer Hill," follow the trail to your left along the ridge. The trail is rutted and there is gopher activity here so watch your footing. After a short steep downhill, turn left and continue straight ahead on the path back toward the base of "Killer Hill." When you're back at the trail to "Killer Hill," turn right to return to the parking lot.

Distance and Difficulty

Jogging and Walking Path
A .5-mile flat path which circles the soccer and softball fields.

Killer Hill Trail
A .8-mile hard packed, somewhat rutted trail for any runner who does not mind a steep uphill.

Safety

The trails are in full view of the park and high school and are well used.

Other Things You Should Know

Parking, restrooms and water fountains are available at the park. Anna Jean Cummings Park is located just north of the Soquel Village on Old San Jose Road. The entrance is just past Soquel High School.

The Soquel High School track is next to the park and offers another cushioned surface on which to run.

ANNA JEAN CUMMINGS PARK

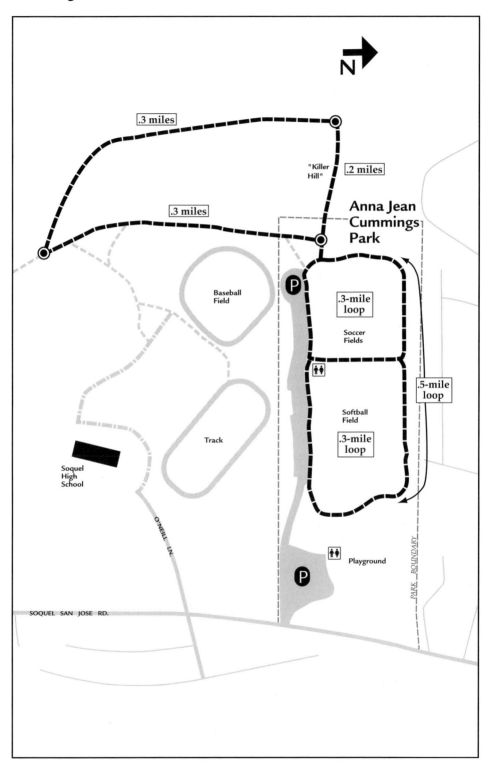

THE FOREST OF NISENE MARKS:
THE LOWER TRAILS

Nisene Marks is a wilderness like none other on the Central Coast. Its miles of trails, the unparalleled beauty, and the unusual calm and quiet under the canopy of the redwoods attract novice and advanced runners alike. The packed dirt trails are well maintained and allow you to keep a good steady pace.

The Forest of Nisene Marks is a 10,000-acre undeveloped state park. It was home to a large-scale lumber operation from 1880 until 1920, when the last of the old growth redwoods were cut. The forest has healed itself and it is hard to believe that this area was so heavily logged less than 100 years ago.

The largest sawmill in Santa Cruz County once stood on Aptos Creek, which runs through Nisene Marks. A company town thrived here, complete with schoolhouse, hotel, telegraph office, and homes and stores for the loggers. A large-gauge and narrow-gauge railroad existed for transporting the lumber. Deep in the canyon a system of levers, pulleys and high wires were used in a precursor to helicopter logging to remove the old growth trees. Remnants of the logging operation and the town can still be seen, and many of the trails follow the old railroad lines with ties still evident in the ground.

Route and Features
George's Picnic Area Loop

The lower trails, including those of the George's Picnic Area Loop, consist of a network of single-track trails which crisscross Aptos Creek. The trailhead is at the entrance station .8 miles into the park on Aptos Creek Road. The road is paved up to this point but the small parking area is dirt. You will find the trailhead to the right of the restroom. From the trail entrance the mild, well-groomed Split Stuff Trail passes by a thicket of blackberry bushes. If the deer have not eaten all of them, the blackberries taste delicious in the midsummer. Bear to your right on the Split Stuff Trail.

At .2 miles the Split Stuff Trail joins the Rancho Aptos Trail. Continue straight ahead on this well-traveled trail. While there are many spurs and mountain bike side trails, you will continue on the main trail which runs between the creek and the road. Continue past the trail marker for the Terrace Trail. At .8 miles you will follow the trail down a steep grade. At the bottom of the hill the trail turns up to the right, but you will cross the creek to your left. There are no bridges here and you will cross on rocks and logs. During the rainy season the creek is often impossible to cross. You will pick up the Vienna Woods Trail on the

(continued on page 73)

Distance and Difficulty

The lower trails consist of easy-to-moderate runs for all level of runners. They are also the only trails in the park open to mountain bikers and horses.

George's Picnic Area Loop
An easy 2.6-mile loop.

Old Growth Loop
An easy loop of 1.5 miles. A seasonal bridge is in place from May to October. From November to April you may not be able to cross the creek.

THE FOREST OF NISENE MARKS: THE LOWER TRAILS

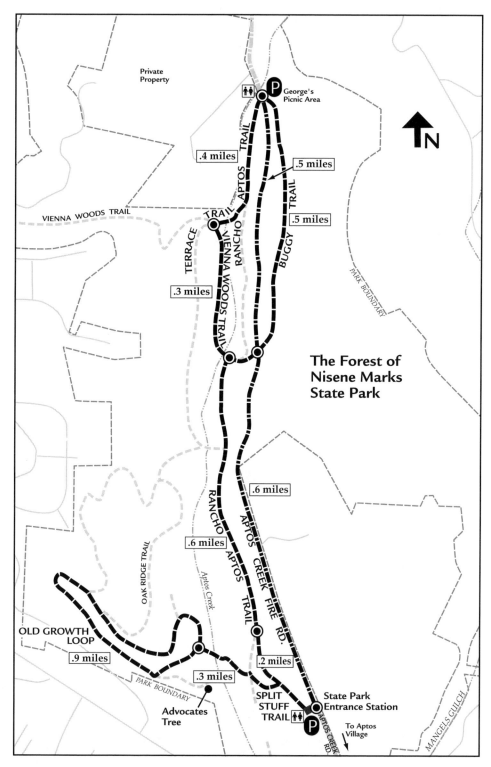

Private Property

George's Picnic Area

.4 miles

.5 miles

.5 miles

N

VIENNA WOODS TRAIL

APTOS TRAIL

RANCHO

BUGGY TRAIL

TERRACE TRAIL

VIENNA WOODS TRAIL

.3 miles

PARK BOUNDARY

The Forest of Nisene Marks State Park

.6 miles

RANCHO APTOS TRAIL

APTOS CREEK FIRE RD.

.6 miles

OAK RIDGE TRAIL

Aptos Creek

OLD GROWTH LOOP

.9 miles

.3 miles

PARK BOUNDARY

Advocates Tree

SPLIT STUFF TRAIL

.2 miles

State Park Entrance Station

APTOS CREEK RD.

To Aptos Village

MANGELS GULCH

Above: Aptos Creek Fire Road travels through the center of the park.

Below: The seasonal bridge along the Old Growth Loop Trail.

other side of the creek . It is to the right of the sandy beach area. Follow the Vienna Woods Trail .3 miles to Terrace Trail. The Vienna Woods Trail is not well marked. It parallels the creek for much of the way and has one mild climb up a rocky hill. At .3 miles it intersects with the Terrace Trail. The intersection can be confusing as there is no trail marker. You will turn right to follow the Terrace Trail down to the creek. If you do make a wrong turn, you will come to a trail marker within a hundred yards for Vienna Woods/Terrace Trail. Simply turn around and continue down to the creek. At the creek crossing there is a seasonal bridge from May-October. Otherwise, you will need to cross on rocks and logs, which can be impossible during the rainy season. After crossing the creek, continue to your left on Terrace Trail as it climbs gradually up a short hill and intersects with Ranch Aptos Trail. Continue up hill to Aptos Creek Fire Road and George's Picnic Area. From George's Picnic Area you can return to the entrance station by way of Aptos Creek Fire Road or you can run back on Buggy Trail. The unmarked Buggy Trail is at the edge of the parking lot where it meets Aptos Creek Fire Road. The trailhead is on your left with the restroom and parking lot behind you. This is a well used trail which has a slight incline and parallels the road. After .5 miles the trail returns to Aptos Creek Fire Road, where you turn left back to the entrance station.

Old Growth Loop

A recent addition to the state park, the land was donated by the Marcel Pourrow family. Follow Split Stuff Trail a few hundred yards to the trail marker intersection. Follow the trail markers to the left to the Old Growth Trail head. This trail takes you around the side of a steep hill. Follow the trail markers carefully for the easiest descent. Cross Rancho Aptos Trail to begin the Old Growth Loop Trail. Cross the seasonal bridge over the Aptos Creek. This crossing is usually impassable when the bridge is down November-April. The trail has many interesting features along the way, including the Twisted Grove of redwood trees, a grove of tiger lilies and, by way of a short detour, the Advocates Tree, which at 250 feet tall is the tallest tree in the park.

. . . .

For additional trail information and a detailed history of the park, we highly recommend Jeff Thomson's book **Explore...The Forest of Nisene Marks State Park**.

Safety

Creek crossings can be difficult and slippery when seasonal bridges are not in place.

We recommend not running alone, staying on trails, and always letting someone know of your planned route.

Watch out for poison oak.

There are no water fountains in the park.

Other Things You Should Know

The road to the entrance of The Forest of Nisene Marks is located in Aptos Village. Turn off Soquel Drive onto Aptos Creek Road at the north entrance to the Aptos Station shops. Cross the railroad tracks and drive past the Aptos Village Park entrance, continuing on Aptos Creek Road .8 miles to the park entrance station. Parking for the lower trails is available at the entrance station and at George's Picnic Area, one mile up the road past the entrance station. User fees are collected in the summer and on weekends throughout the year. There are outhouses in both parking areas.

THE FOREST OF NISENE MARKS:
THE UPPER TRAILS

The rugged and scenic upper trails offer magnificent vistas and a variety of historic ruins. Hoffman's Historic Site, the best preserved of the local ruins, was a large logging camp in use from 1918-1921. Sand Point Overlook, at an elevation of 1600 feet, offers wonderful views of the bay and the southern parts of Santa Cruz County. The Forest of Nisene Marks is also famous as the epicenter of the 1989 Loma Prieta earthquake. A marker on the Aptos Creek Trail commemorates the site.

Routes and Features

You will be running on single-track trails. Even on the hottest days you are in a cool, shady, damp forest. On Sunday mornings in particular, these trails, while never crowded, are well traveled by runners and hikers. Bicycles and horses are not allowed.

West Ridge Trail Loop

At 2.3 miles from Soquel Drive on Aptos Creek Fire Road, one half mile past George's Picnic Area (at the dip in the road just past the steel bridge), there is a trailhead marker on the left hand side. This is the beginning of West Ridge Trail. Entering the trail, you'll travel a short distance along a branch creek before crossing it and beginning your upward climb. The crossing is always passable. The trail ascends, sometimes steeply, to the power poles, where you will get a narrow view over to the Felton sand mines and across to Trout Gulch. The trail continues along the ridge through oak and redwood forest a total of 4.3 miles. There is one steep, step-like climb along this section and most of the way it is uphill. At the Ridge Connection Trail you turn right .4 miles to meet Loma Prieta Grade Trail, also known as Hoffman's. Hoffman's is an historic area of old shacks, stores and outhouses, the dilapidated remains of which are still visible. Loma Prieta Trail drops through a steep short section here that is quite rutted. After passing through Hoffman's Historic Site, you will continue down the trail laid along the old railroad tracks. The trail ends in 2.3 miles at Aptos Creek Fire Road. Turn right on the road to the locked gate and continue around it on the road back to the start.

Sand Point via West Ridge or Hoffman's

Follow the directions for the West Ridge Loop above. At 4.3 miles, instead of turning right on the Ridge Connection Trail as above, bear left to continue up West Ridge Trail. This section of the trail leads you out of the redwood forest into a completely different ecosystem of madrone and shrubs and full exposure to the sun. You will also have spectacular views of Monterey Bay and the entire canyon of Aptos Creek. 1.9 miles from the intersection with the Ridge Connection Trail, West Ridge Trail ends at Hinckley Fire Road and the West Ridge trail camp, where there

(continued on page 76)

Distance and Difficulty

With the exception of the Mill Pond Trail loop, these trails are best suited for well-conditioned trail runners. They are rugged and isolated, and there is an elevation gain of up to 1800 feet. However, the surface is good and these are considered the best running trails in the county.

West Ridge Trail Loop
A strenuous 8.4-mile loop.

Sand Point via the West Ridge Trail or Hoffman's
An extremely strenuous 13.4-mile or 11.4-mile loop.

Mill Pond Trail
A 1.6-mile easy loop of mostly flat running

Bridge Creek Trail
A strenuous 6-mile loop.

Aptos Creek Trail
An adventurous, strenuous loop of 11.9 or 10.5 miles.

THE FOREST OF NISENE MARKS: THE UPPER TRAILS

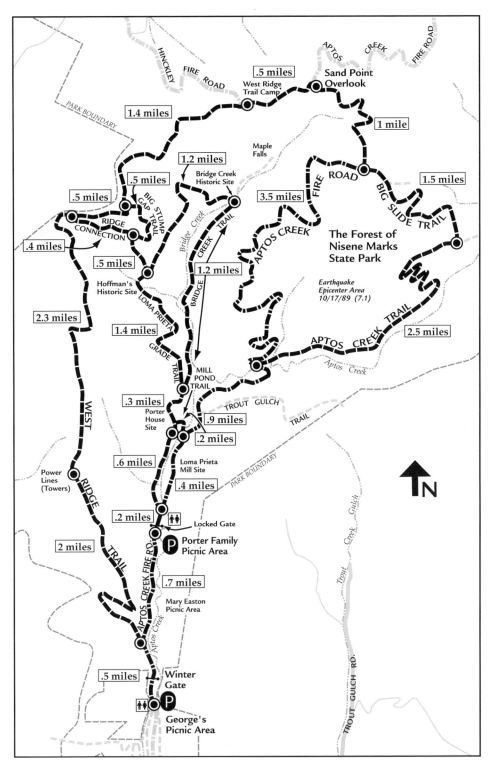

Sand Point Overlook

.5 miles

West Ridge Trail Camp

1.4 miles

1 mile

HINCKLEY FIRE ROAD

APTOS CREEK FIRE ROAD

PARK BOUNDARY

Maple Falls

1.2 miles

Bridge Creek Historic Site

.5 miles

.5 miles

BIG STUMP GAP TRAIL

RIDGE CONNECTION

.4 miles

.5 miles

Hoffman's Historic Site

LOMA PRIETA

1.4 miles

GRADE TRAIL

2.3 miles

WEST

1.2 miles

BRIDGE CREEK TRAIL

3.5 miles

1.5 miles

APTOS CREEK

FIRE ROAD

BIG SLIDE TRAIL

The Forest of Nisene Marks State Park

Earthquake Epicenter Area 10/17/89 (7.1)

2.5 miles

APTOS CREEK TRAIL

Aptos Creek

MILL POND TRAIL

TROUT GULCH TRAIL

.3 miles

Porter House Site

.9 miles

.2 miles

.6 miles

Loma Prieta Mill Site

RIDGE

Power Lines (Towers)

2 miles

PARK BOUNDARY

.4 miles

N

Trout Creek Gulch

.2 miles

Locked Gate

P Porter Family Picnic Area

TRAIL

APTOS CREEK FIRE RD.

.7 miles

Mary Easton Picnic Area

Aptos Creek

.5 miles

Winter Gate

P George's Picnic Area

TROUT GULCH RD.

is an outhouse. Turn right on the road and run .5 miles up to the great view at Sand Point Overlook. Then continue on a long, relentless, pounding run down the hill on Aptos Creek Fire Road back to the locked gate. Pass around the gate and continue to the trailhead. Many runners prefer this route in the reverse. It is easier to come down the trail, which goes up and down, rather than down the continuous and hard-packed descent of the fire road.

You can also begin this loop at the locked gate near the Porter Family Picnic area parking lot 3 miles up Aptos Creek Fire Road. From here, run up the Loma Prieta Grade Trail, locally known as Hoffman's, 2.5 miles to Hoffman's Historic Site. Continue on Loma Prieta Grade Trail .5 miles to Big Stump Gap Trail. This trail meets West Ridge Trail after .5 miles. Turn right on West Ridge Trail to proceed to Sand Point as above. The total mileage for this loop is 11.4 miles.

Mill Pond Trail

This loop begins at the locked gate near the Porter Family Picnic area on Aptos Creek Fire Road three miles from Soquel Drive. After .2 miles on Aptos Creek Fire Road turn left onto the well marked Loma Prieta Grade Trail. This flat, well maintained trail with easy footing follows the old railroad line and winds through the redwood forest. You will pass the Porter House Site. Historical markers and displays describe the home and ranch buildings that once existed in this now pristine spot. Just past the Porter House Site, turn right at the Mill Pond Trail (once known as Schoolhouse Trail) and run down the trail to the bridge which crosses the creek. After crossing the bridge the trail meets the Aptos Creek Fire Road, which is closed to traffic here. Turn right. You will pass the Loma Prieta Mill Site with historical markers and photos detailing the town that once stood here. Continue on the road back to the parking area.

Bridge Creek Trail

Bridge Creek is thought by many to be the most beautiful trail in the park. Begin at the locked gate 3 miles from Soquel Drive on Aptos Creek Fire Road. There is parking here. At .2 miles, take the Loma Prieta Trail to your left. Continue .9 miles to the intersection with Bridge Creek Trail. Follow the right fork straight ahead. The trail runs along Bridge Creek for 1.2 miles. It is a narrow trail, which goes up and down and around trees, but the footing is quite good. The trail still shows evidence of the storms of 1983 when the creek was blocked with fallen trees and then let loose with a roar, taking out everything in its path. If you look up the sides of the canyon, you can see the high water line where the sides of the canyon slid. You will reach the marker for the Bridge Creek Historic Site, although there are no longer any ruins to be seen. Cross the creek. The trail continues on the other side. The creek is almost always passable on logs or stones. Once you cross the creek, you will go up what is locally known as "The Ski Jump" or "Elevator." This description will give you an idea of the length and steepness of the climb. If you can

Safety

The upper trails in the park are isolated. We recommended that you not run alone, especially on weekdays when the park is not well used. Although there is no record of mountain lions being spotted in Nisene Marks, it is mountain lion habitat. Watch for poison oak, especially on West Ridge Trail, and use appropriate precautions if necessary.

Carry water.
There is no water past the fountain in the parking lot of Aptos Station. These trails are deceiving and they will take you much longer than the equivalent miles on the road.

Stay on trails.
From time to time there have been reports of runners and hikers becoming lost in Nisene Marks. Stay on the trails, always tell someone of your planned route, and stick to your plan. Start early enough in the day to have plenty of time to finish before dark.

run all the way up, you are in great shape! At 1.2 miles from the creek crossing you will pass through Hoffman's Historic Site. From Hoffman's it is 1.4 miles back to the intersection with Bridge Creek Trail. Retrace your steps to Aptos Creek Fire Road and turn right to reach the parking lot.

Aptos Creek Trail Loop

Formerly a rarely used trail, and then only by the most dedicated wilderness runners and hikers, the Aptos Creek Trail has become popular as the route to the epicenter of the 1989 Loma Prieta earthquake. The epicenter is marked with a sign. Although the trees have filled back in since the earthquake, in the years immediately following the quake, hikers and runners could look up and see where the force of the quake snapped off the redwood tops. To reach Aptos Creek Trail, begin at the locked gate on Aptos Creek Fire Road, 3 miles in from Soquel Drive. Run on the road for 1.5 miles. You will pass the Old Mill Site where the lumber operation had its headquarters, saw mill and a small village. The fire road runs along a branch of Aptos Creek, and while wide it is closed to all traffic except the occasional park ranger. The Big Slide trailhead is found just after crossing the footbridge. The well marked trail is on the right side of the road. Upon entering the trail you will immediately descend steeply for 20 yards to the creek crossing. This crossing is virtually impassable during the rainy season. At other times of the year you will need to cross on stones and boulders.

The run to the epicenter is relatively mild. You will be on a narrow single-track trail through a woods and meadow area and then come to your second creek crossing. This crossing is much easier than the first as the boulders you will scramble over are quite large and raised out of the water. In a few hundred more yards you will be at the epicenter. From here the trail becomes an adventure. It traverses several slides and washouts. After several of these crossings you will begin a series of switchbacks which will bring you high up the creek canyon. At the top of the switchbacks you will continue up a mild incline. Aptos Creek Trail joins Big Slide Trail which travels through a fairy tale-like land of marshes and ponds that are sometimes dry and sometimes full and covered with algae. The trail stays dry throughout. The trail ends back at Aptos Creek Fire Road, at which point you can turn right up to Sand Point Overlook (1600' elevation) and come back down on the West Ridge and Loma Prieta Trails for a distance of 11.9 miles (see the West Ridge Trail description on page 74). You can also turn left and come back down Aptos Creek Fire Road (for a distance of 10.5 miles).

Other Things You Should Know

Parking for the upper trails is available at George's Picnic Area, 1.8 miles up Aptos Creek Fire Road and at the Porter Family Picnic Area, 3 miles up the road. At George's Picnic Area there is a gate which is often locked during the rainy winter months. Cars cannot proceed further. There are also a couple of spaces at the West Ridge trailhead 2.3 miles up Aptos Creek Road. User fees are collected in the summer and on weekends throughout the year. There are outhouses at the parking lots, at the Mary Easton Picnic Area and at West Ridge Trail Camp.

SANTA CRUZ COUNTY BEACHES:
DESCRIPTIONS AND DISTANCES

Unlike most of the world, those of us who live in Santa Cruz can choose to run on a variety of beautiful beaches. Running on sand can be a good variation to your running routine. You get a slower but harder workout, plus the extra effort involved in keeping your balance on the uneven surface tends to work your entire body. People with ankle, knee or hip problems should probably talk to their doctor to make sure they won't aggravate any injuries.

The distances displayed on the maps are approximate, since the season and tides can greatly influence the size of the beaches.

Santa Cruz Beach and Cowell Beach
Santa Cruz Beach, often referred to as Boardwalk Beach or Main Beach, runs from the mouth of the San Lorenzo River to the Santa Cruz Municipal Wharf. Cowell Beach is the small beach that runs from the wharf to the cliffs next to the Coast Santa Cruz Hotel. The Santa Cruz Beach Boardwalk was built in 1907 by Fred W. Swanton and is the oldest amusement park in California.

The distance from the wharf to the cliffs is .2 miles and the distance from the mouth of the San Lorenzo River to the wharf is .6 miles.

There is metered parking available along Beach Street and the streets intersecting it.

Seabright Beach
Once called Castle Beach because of the castle-like building that stood on East Cliff near the intersection of Mott Street, Seabright Beach runs from San Lorenzo Point (at the mouth of the San Lorenzo River) to the yacht harbor jetty. Seabright Beach takes its name from the surrounding neighborhood, which was developed by F.M. Mott in 1884. He named it after a village he had visited in New Jersey called Sea Bright. Seabright Beach is now officially part of Twin Lakes State Beach.

The distance from San Lorenzo Point to the jetty is .5 miles.

There is limited parking in the neighborhoods surrounding Seabright Beach and some metered parking available on the west side of the yacht harbor.

Twin Lakes Beach
Woods Lagoon (which has now become the yacht harbor) and Schwan Lagoon were known as the Twin Lakes, and the surrounding area became know as the Twin Lakes neighborhood. In 1955 the state established Twin Lakes State Beach. While the official beach includes Seabright Beach, most locals consider Twin Lakes to be the small beach south of the yacht harbor in front of Schwan Lake.

(continued on page 80)

SANTA CRUZ COUNTY BEACHES

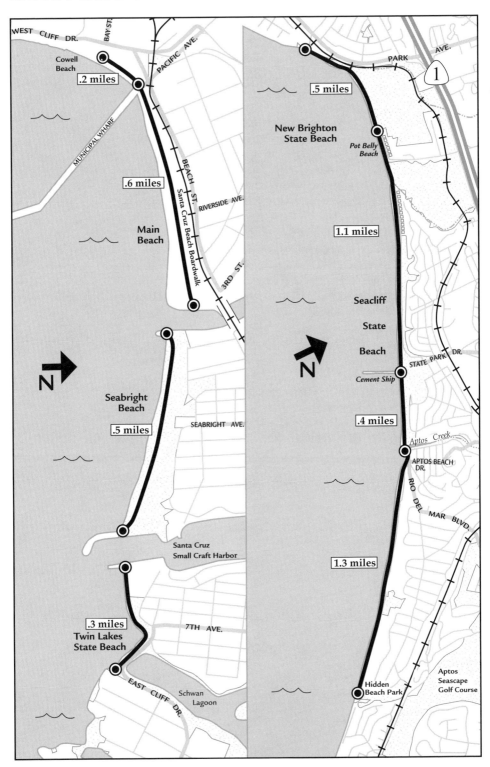

Cowell Beach

.2 miles

WEST CLIFF DR.

BAY ST.

PACIFIC AVE.

MUNICIPAL WHARF

.6 miles

BEACH ST.

Santa Cruz Beach Boardwalk

RIVERSIDE AVE.

Main Beach

3RD ST.

Seabright Beach

.5 miles

SEABRIGHT AVE.

Santa Cruz Small Craft Harbor

.3 miles
Twin Lakes State Beach

7TH AVE.

EAST CLIFF DR.

Schwan Lagoon

PARK AVE.

.5 miles

New Brighton State Beach

Pot Belly Beach

1.1 miles

Seacliff State Beach

STATE PARK DR.

Cement Ship

.4 miles

Aptos Creek

APTOS BEACH DR.

RIO DEL MAR BLVD.

1.3 miles

Hidden Beach Park

Aptos Seascape Golf Course

1

The beach is about .3 miles long, although its size varies significantly during the seasons. In the winter months it is difficult to run past the point. During the summer you can run as far as 16th Avenue.

There is limited parking along East Cliff, and fee or metered parking is available at the yacht harbor parking lots.

New Brighton and Seacliff State Beaches

In the late 1870's Thomas Fallon established a resort next to the railroad tracks on the bluff above the current New Brighton Beach State Park. He built a hotel on the property called the New Brighton, which eventually gave the area its name. New Brighton Beach State Park was established in 1933. The western part of New Brighton Beach was formerly known as China Beach after the small village of Chinese fishermen who lived there in the 1870s and 1880s.

Between New Brighton and Seacliff State Beaches are Potbelly Beach, which fronts 16 private beach homes, the undeveloped Porter Sesnon property, and Las Olas Beach. (Las Olas was sometimes called "hard floor beach" by locals because the homes along Las Olas were fancier than those at Pot Belly Beach.)

Seacliff State Beach was established in 1931. Its most famous and prominent feature is the cement ship Palo Alto. Built as a tanker and launched in 1919 after the end of WWI, it never saw service and was sold in 1930 to the Cal-Neva Company. Towed to Seacliff and connected by a pier to the shore, it had a brief life as an amusement center. Ravaged by storms over the years, it is no longer accessible to the public. A one-way run from the cliffs at New Brighton Beach to Hidden Beach Park is 3.3 miles. Refer to the map for shorter routes.

SANTA CRUZ:
A GUIDE FOR RUNNERS, JOGGERS AND SERIOUS WALKERS

POPULAR RACE ROUTES

WHARF TO WHARF

For over 30 years the Wharf to Wharf has been drawing runners from all over the world to Santa Cruz. *Runner's World* magazine called this six-mile run "the best little road race in California." Run every year on the fourth Sunday in July, its scenic route along the coast, coupled with the cool summer weather and festive atmosphere, make it a wonderful race for both casual joggers and serious runners.

Description

Racers congregate for the start in Santa Cruz along Beach Street between the Santa Cruz Municipal Wharf and the Santa Cruz Beach Boardwalk. Over 14,000 runners line up, with the elite runners up front and the rest stretched out over a few hundred yards loosely organized by average pace. The race begins with runners heading down Beach Street, past the roller coaster, then down to and across the San Lorenzo Bridge. Unless you are part of the elite group up front, the first mile of the race is a mass of humanity, and a slow jog is the best you can hope for. The crowds gradually thin as the race continues along East Cliff, past the yacht harbor and along the loop around Twin Lakes Beach and Schwan Lake. Just before 17th Avenue, East Cliff turns toward the bay and heads toward the scenic cliffs and neighborhoods of Pleasure Point. The last half mile is a gradual downhill to the finish at the Capitola Wharf.

There are only two short uphill sections of the race, both coming early in the run. The first comes in the first mile as you ascend East Cliff up to the Seabright neighborhood, the second as you loop around Schwan Lake past Twin Lakes Beach. There is also an uphill from Corcoran Lagoon towards Pleasure Point, but it is so gradual that it goes almost unnoticed.

Safety

This race is extremely crowded and you have to carefully watch for other runners – both those you are passing and those trying to pass you. Unless you try to run with the elite runners up front, you have to consider this a "fun run" and adjust your pace to run with the crowd.

Other Things You Should Know

Registration for the Wharf to Wharf usually begins in April and sells out long before the race. There is no race-day registration. Registration forms and other information can be found at www.wharftowharf.com. Race proceeds benefit Santa Cruz County youth sports and the running community.

©John Hilmer 2004

WHARF TO WHARF

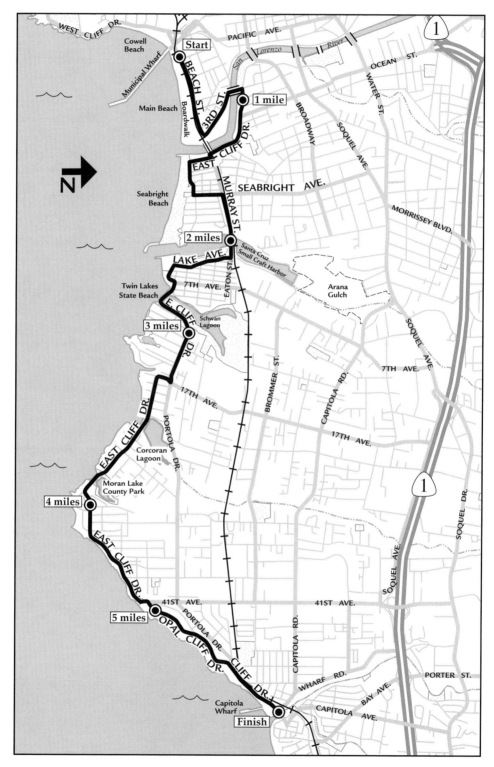

TURKEY TROT AND SUPER BOWL RUN

The Turkey Trot is run on the Saturday before Thanksgiving and is a good way to work off extra calories before your Thanksgiving feast. The Turkey trot offers the choice of a 5K, 10K or kids' 1K race. Overall winners get a turkey, and awards go out to top finishers in each age and gender division.

Description

The Turkey Trot is a flat, out-and-back course on the path along West Cliff Drive. The races begin on Delaware Street near the back of Natural Bridges State Park. The kids' 1K is usually run first, followed by the 5K and the 10K. Typically 150-200 runners compete in the 5K, and 250 run the 10K race. The course follows Delaware to Swanton to West Cliff. After a few miles on West Cliff, runners turn around and retrace their steps. It is a good opportunity for slower runners to see the fast runners in action (and vice versa).

This is a beautiful course. Weather is usually mild, and the race is normally early enough in the day for there to be little wind.

. . . .

The Super Bowl Run is identical to the Turkey Trot except that it is run every year on Super Bowl Sunday and a 3k race is offered instead of a 5k. It benefits the Special Olympics. Both the Turkey Trot and Super Bowl Run are sponsored by the Santa Cruz Track Club.

Safety

The first and last part of the race travels along Delaware Avenue and Swanton Boulevard. Since the roads are not closed off, you have to be aware of the occasional car or truck.

Other Things You Should Know

Race registration for the Turkey Trot usually begins in October and in January for the Super Bowl Run (although many people will register the day of the races). More information (including race results from prior years) can be found on the Santa Cruz Track Club website: www.sctc.runners.net.

TURKEY TROT AND SUPER BOWL RUN

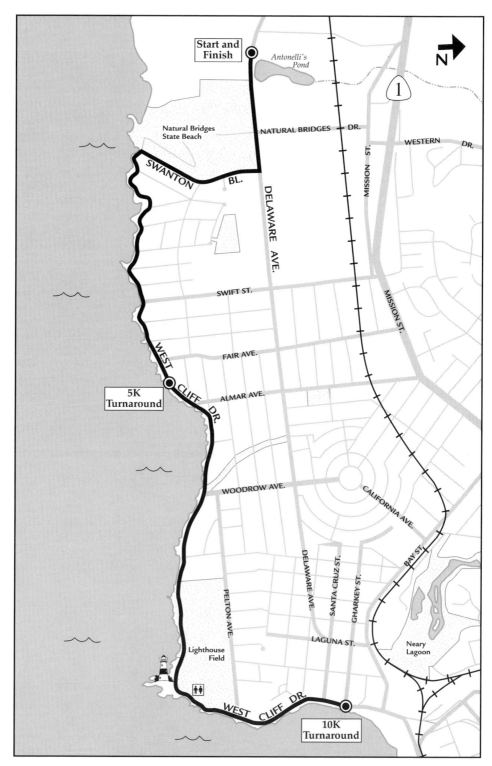

Start and Finish

Antonelli's Pond

N

1

Natural Bridges State Beach

NATURAL BRIDGES — DR.

WESTERN — DR.

SWANTON — BL.

DELAWARE — AVE.

MISSION — ST.

SWIFT ST.

MISSION — ST.

WEST — CLIFF — DR.

FAIR AVE.

5K Turnaround

ALMAR AVE.

WOODROW AVE.

CALIFORNIA — AVE.

BAY ST.

DELAWARE — AVE.

SANTA CRUZ ST.

GHARKEY ST.

PELTON — AVE.

Lighthouse Field

LAGUNA ST.

Neary Lagoon

WEST — CLIFF — DR.

10K Turnaround

FIRECRACKER 10K

The Firecracker 10k, run on the Fourth of July, is currently sponsored by the Sunrise Rotary Club. The course is very challenging, featuring a mix of cross country and road racing.

Description

The course begins at Harvey West Park. It covers two miles on flat asphalt roads and then climbs through Pogonip. Here the course meanders through a grassy meadow, steeply ascends a rocky dirt road, and flattens out onto a dirt fire road. It then returns to the asphalt road and travels through the upper Spring Street neighborhood before taking a corkscrew turn down a steep hill onto a bike path into Harvey West.

Other Things You Should Know

The race has been run for over 20 years. It is well organized with plenty of volunteers to direct runners and distribute water. The sweatshirts awarded to top finishers are coveted awards among Santa Cruz runners. There are restrooms at the start and finish but none along the course. A pancake breakfast follows the race and is free to all runners. More information about the Firecracker 10K can be found on the Santa Cruz Track Club website: www.sctc.runners.net.

FIRECRACKER 10K

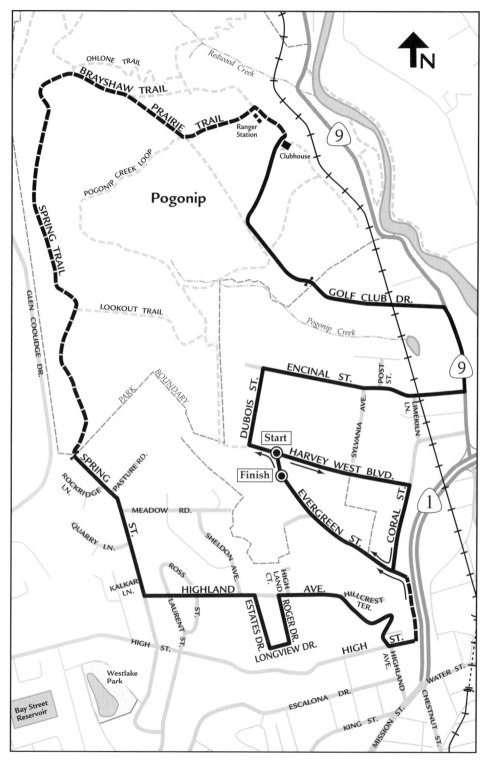

APTOS WOMEN'S 5-MILER

The Aptos Women's 5-Miler was begun in 1981 and has attracted crowds of women each year. It is one of the few remaining all-women races in the county. It is usually run on the second Sunday in June. The race is known for the camaraderie and support of women and running. Many women have run their first race here.

Description

The race begins and ends at the Aptos Village Park, which is located below the Aptos Station shops in the village of Aptos. After a short but steep hill in the first .25 miles, the course becomes flat as it travels Aptos Creek Fire Road inside Nisene Marks State Park. Following the U-turn at the halfway mark, the course continues on the single track Buggy Trail before rejoining the fire road for the return to the start.

Other Things You Should Know

A highlight of the race is the seemingly endless raffle of prizes donated by local merchants held at its conclusion.

Proceeds from the race are donated to Advocates for Nisene Marks, the Santa Cruz Track Club and the Santa Cruz Track Youth Club. More information about the race can be found on the Santa Cruz Track Club website: www.sctc.runners.net.

Courtesy Ron Austin

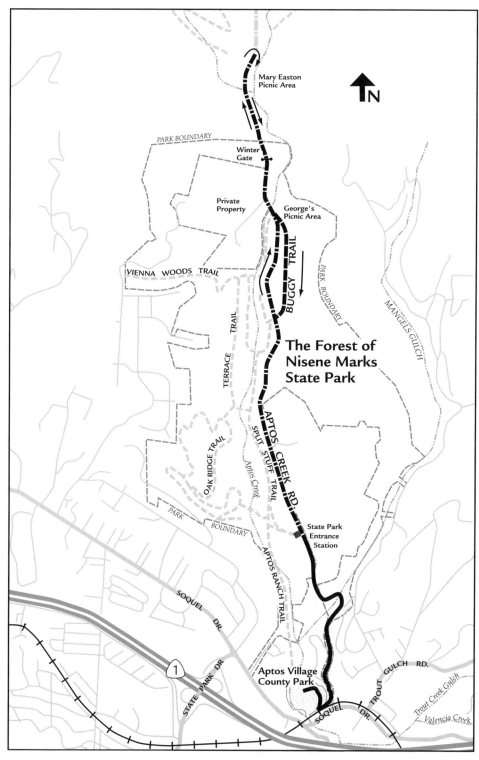

Mary Easton
Picnic Area

N

PARK BOUNDARY

Winter
Gate

Private
Property

George's
Picnic Area

VIENNA WOODS TRAIL

BUGGY TRAIL

PARK BOUNDARY

MANGELS GULCH

The Forest of
Nisene Marks
State Park

TERRACE TRAIL

APTOS CREEK RD.

SPLIT STUFF TRAIL

OAK RIDGE TRAIL

Aptos Creek

PARK BOUNDARY

State Park
Entrance
Station

APTOS RANCH TRAIL

SOQUEL DR.

STATE PARK DR.

1

Aptos Village
County Park

GULCH RD.

TROUT CREEK

SOQUEL DR.

Trout Creek Gulch

Valencia Creek

THE CARDIAC PACER

The Cardiac Pacer is the oldest continuously run cross country race in Santa Cruz County. Begun in 1977, the Pacer is run twice a year, usually in April and November. The number of runners has ranged from 2 to 94 over the history of the race. The no-frills Cardiac Pacer continues a tradition of pure fun and love of running.

Description

This challenging, cross-country five-mile race begins at the UCSC track and winds its way across campus, up stairs, around fences, over bridges and into the Natural Reserve. The course is accurately measured and generally marked, but there are no course marshals and it is sometimes difficult to find your way. Study the map before you begin and keep another runner in sight. There is no water on the course but plenty at the finish.

The infamous inscribed bananas await the top ten men and women at the finish. The course has remained remarkably true to the original, changing only as natural reserve regulations and campus construction warrants. The entry fee of $2-$5 is a far cry from $25, $35 and even $50 it now costs to enter most races. There are runners who return every year to the race and each year new runners join the faithful. For more information, contact the OPERS Intramural Sports Program at UCSC at (831) 459-4220 or send a email to kdgivens@ucsc.edu.

Other Things You Should Know

The race is a throwback to the origins of the running movement when friends would meet, sometimes pay a few dollars for an entry fee, and run on a measured course. Refreshments usually were served but sponsors, fundraisers, t-shirts and even trophies or medals were unheard of. Runners ran for the fun of running and testing themselves against the clock and each other.

THE CARDIAC PACER

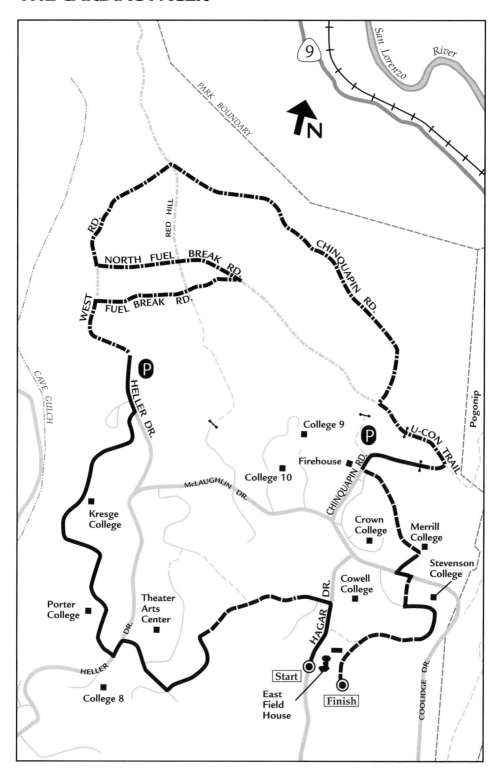

THE UCSC SLUG RUN

A relatively recent addition to the Santa Cruz racing scene is the UCSC Slug Run. Named after the school mascot, the race was begun to bring attention and funds to the UCSC cross country team. Begun in 2000, the race adds a spring opportunity for locals to test their fitness.

The Slug Run offers a 10K, 5K and half-mile for kids 12 and under. The 10K covers a difficult course with steep hills, grassy fields, dirt trails and many twists and turns.

Description

The Slug Run begins on the athletic fields and winds its way through the colleges and onto the fire roads of the UCSC Campus Natural Reserve. The 5K also begins on the athletic field and steeply descends and ascends the outer boundaries of the athletic fields and pastures. For more information, contact The OPERS Intramural Sports Program at UCSC at 831-459-4220 or send a message to kdgivens@ucsc.edu.

Both the 5K and 10K courses offer magnificent views of the university, the city of Santa Cruz, and the Monterey Bay. The races are well organized by the UCSC cross country team. Many monitors on the courses cheer runners on and ensure that no one makes a wrong turn.

THE UCSC SLUG RUN: 5K

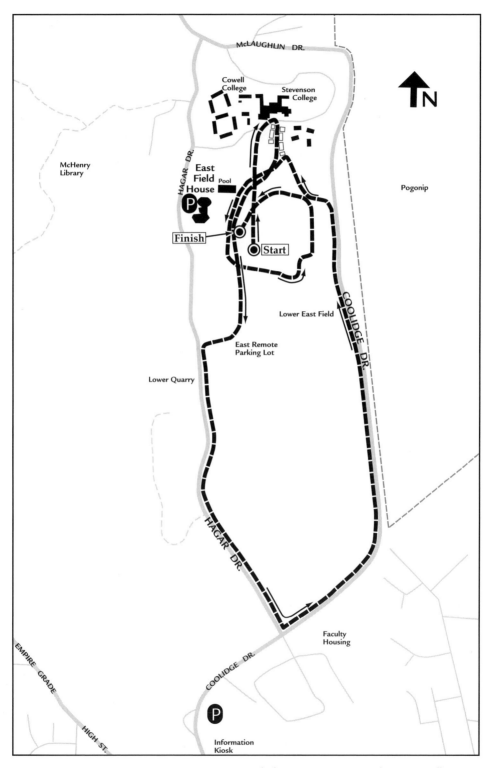

THE UCSC SLUG RUN: 10K

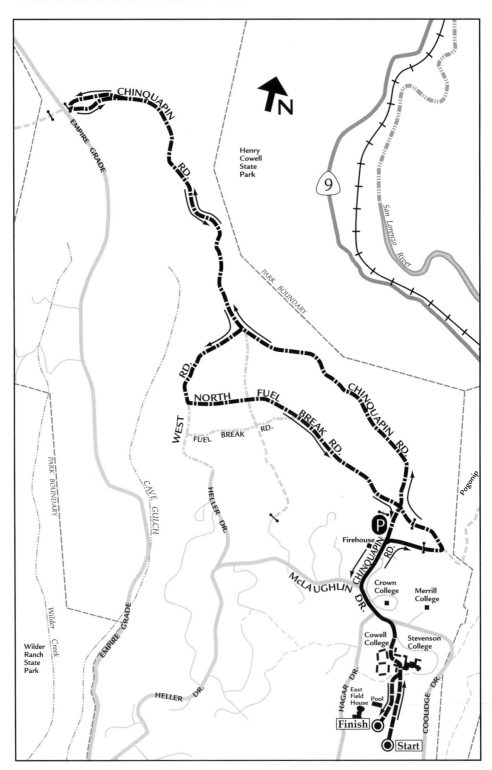

OTHER SANTA CRUZ AREA RACES

There are many other well-organized races in the Santa Cruz area which you may wish to run. Although we are unable to list all of them, here are a few of special interest.

The **PAJARO VALLEY RUN FOR SHELTER** is a benefit for the Pajaro Valley Shelter Services. It is run on Mother's Day each year and features a 10K, 5K and 1K children's run. It is run through and around the city of Watsonville. Contact www.sctc.runners.net or www.pvshelter.org for more information.

The **RACE THRU THE REDWOODS 10K** is held in downtown Felton and Henry Cowell Redwoods State Park. It has been run for over 30 years and features road and trail running with steep climbs. It is known for its small town feel and camaraderie. It is run in August. You can register at www.racethrutheredwoods.com.

The **NISENE MARKS MARATHON, HALF-MARATHON AND 5K** is run on the first Saturday of June. Known for its rugged trail running, it is a favorite with ultra runners. Registration is limited and usually sells out for the marathon and half-marathon. Check the Sponsored Races section at www.sctc.runners.net for more information.

Other Things You Should Know

An expanded listing of local races (including race results) can be found on the Santa Cruz Track Club website. Go to www.sctc.runners.net.

"It's a beautiful day in the neighborhood."

MILEAGE MAPS FOR SANTA CRUZ NEIGHBORHOODS

Recognizing that many people like to jog in and around their neighborhood and would like to be able to estimate the distance that they have run, we have included maps of selected North Santa Cruz County neighborhoods highlighting key streets with distances marked. If you run on a nearby street, the mileages may help you "estimate" the length of your specific run. Distances between markers have been rounded to the nearest tenth of a mile.

The streets highlighted have been selected for mileage purposes only. Many have heavy traffic and/or no sidewalks. As with all urban or neighborhood running, when choosing a running route, consider traffic and safety issues and be cautious.

WEST SANTA CRUZ MILEAGE MAP

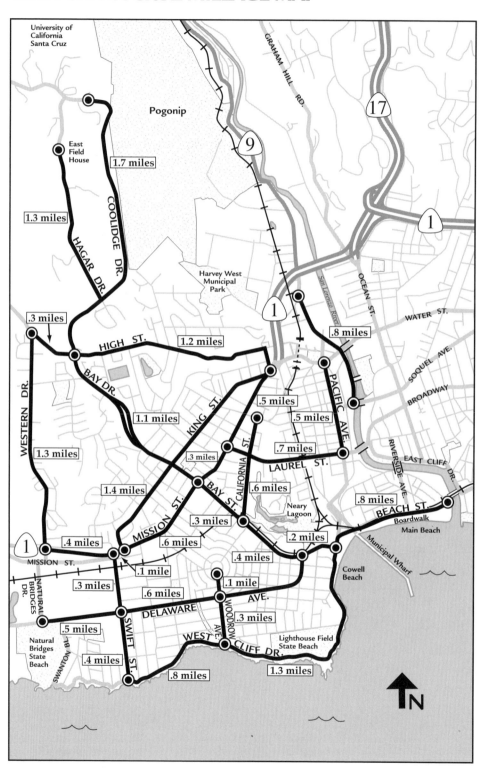

University of California Santa Cruz

Pogonip

East Field House

1.7 miles

1.3 miles

COOLIDGE DR.

HAGAR DR.

GRAHAM HILL RD.

9

17

1

Harvey West Municipal Park

San Lorenzo River

.3 miles

HIGH ST.

1.2 miles

1

.8 miles

WATER ST.

OCEAN ST.

SOQUEL AVE.

BROADWAY

BAY DR.

WESTERN DR.

1.1 miles

KING ST.

.5 miles

.5 miles

PACIFIC AVE.

1.3 miles

.3 miles

CALIFORNIA ST.

.7 miles

LAUREL ST.

RIVERSIDE AVE.

EAST CLIFF DR.

1.4 miles

BAY ST.

.6 miles

Neary Lagoon

.8 miles

BEACH ST.

Boardwalk

Main Beach

MISSION ST.

.3 miles

.2 miles

1

.4 miles

MISSION ST.

.6 miles

.4 miles

Cowell Beach

Municipal Wharf

.1 mile

NATURAL BRIDGES DR.

.3 miles

.6 miles

.1 mile

WOODROW AVE.

AVE.

SWANTON BL.

.5 miles

SWIFT ST.

DELAWARE

WEST CLIFF DR.

.3 miles

Lighthouse Field State Beach

Natural Bridges State Beach

.4 miles

.8 miles

1.3 miles

N

EAST SANTA CRUZ MILEAGE MAP

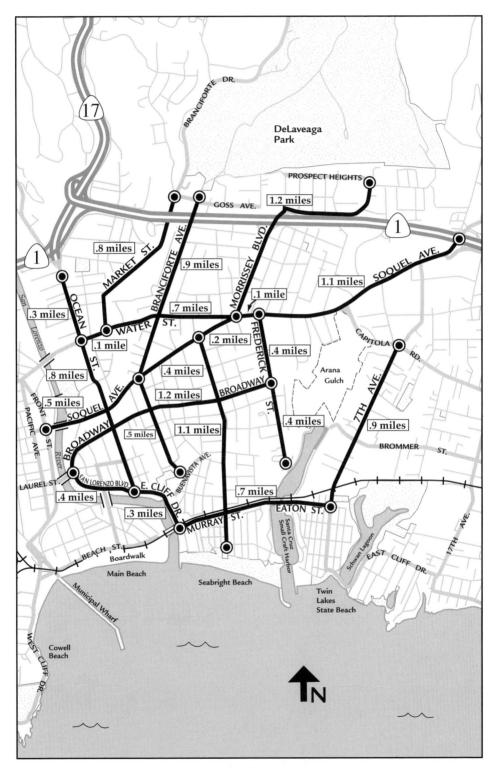

LIVE OAK/PLEASURE POINT MILEAGE MAP

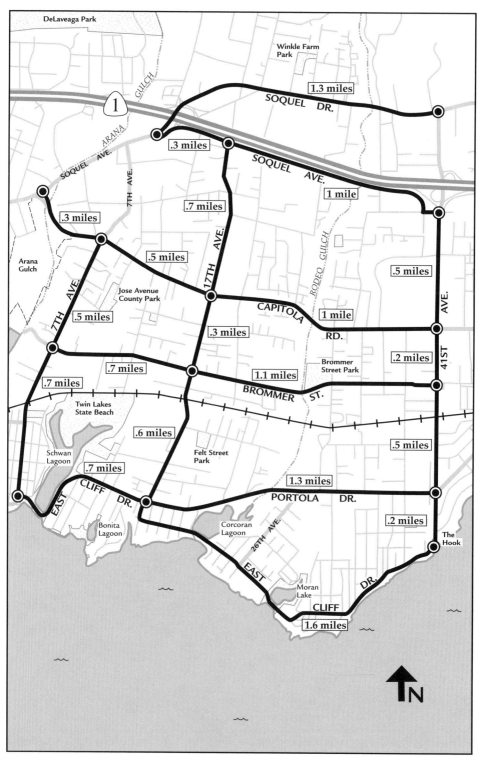

CAPITOLA/SOQUEL MILEAGE MAP

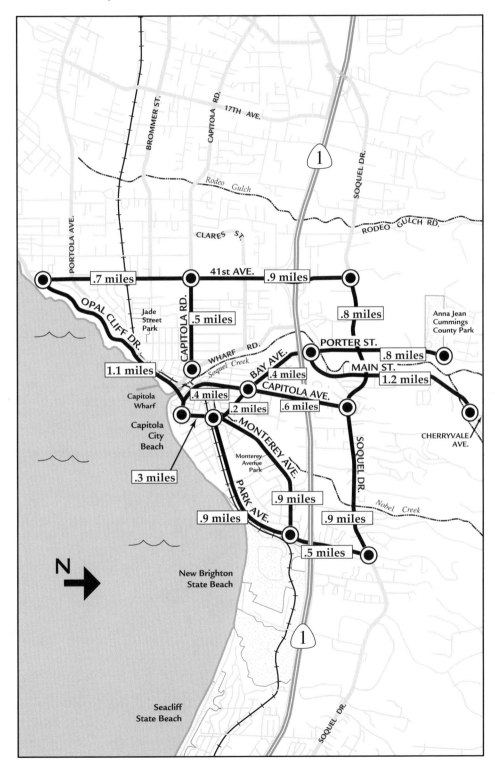

APTOS/RIO DEL MAR MILEAGE MAP

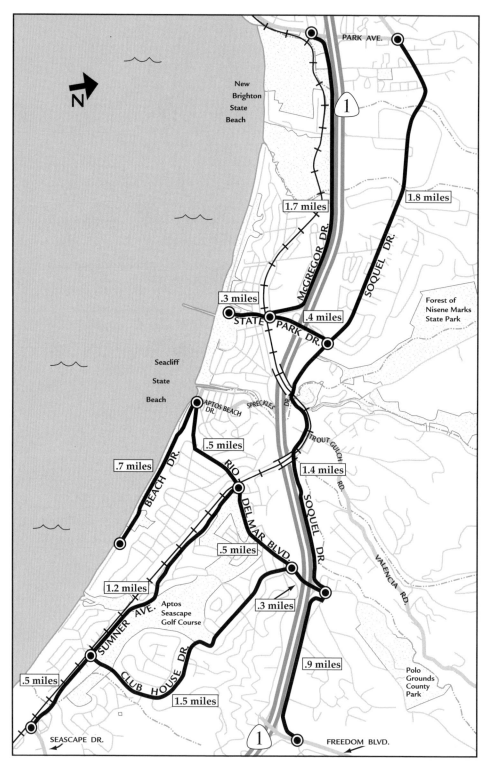

New Brighton State Beach

PARK AVE.

1

McGREGOR DR.

SOQUEL DR.

1.7 miles

1.8 miles

Forest of Nisene Marks State Park

.3 miles

STATE PARK DR.

.4 miles

Seacliff State Beach

APTOS BEACH DR.

SPRECKLES DR.

.5 miles

TROUT GULCH RD.

1.4 miles

.7 miles

BEACH DR.

RIO DEL MAR BLVD.

SOQUEL DR.

.5 miles

VALENCIA RD.

1.2 miles

Aptos Seascape Golf Course

.3 miles

.9 miles

Polo Grounds County Park

SUMNER AVE.

CLUB HOUSE DR.

.5 miles

1.5 miles

SEASCAPE DR.

1

FREEDOM BLVD.

SANTA CRUZ:
A GUIDE FOR RUNNERS, JOGGERS AND SERIOUS WALKERS

·····································

APPENDICES

RUNNING OR WALKING WITH YOUR DOG

Taking your canine pal along on your runs or walks can be a great benefit for you both. Dogs are good companions and many dogs love running. For high-energy dogs, running is a good way to incorporate the exercise they need into your regular routine. And because of the usually temperate weather, Santa Cruz can be an especially good place to run or walk with dogs. Many of the routes listed in this book are dog friendly, though others (notably parks and greenbelt areas) have some restrictions about where you can take your dog. Trails and areas open to dogs often change; refer to trail signs for current information.

A Few Good Places to Take Your Dog

POGONIP: Pogonip is a very popular dog walking and running area. Dogs are allowed on several trails, including the Spring Trail. They are not allowed in sensitive habitat areas.

HENRY COWELL STATE PARK: Pipeline Road is open to dogs. This access road has plenty of space for you and your dog to run or walk side by side. Dogs are not allowed on most of the side trails.

FOREST OF NISENE MARKS STATE PARK: Aptos Creek Fire Road and many of the smaller trails in lower Nisene Marks are open to dogs. Nisene Marks can be a cool spot to walk or run on even the warmest days. Upper trails are not open to dogs.

SANTA CRUZ YACHT HARBOR: With Frederick Street Park at one end of the harbor, and the beach at the other, on this route you can easily incorporate doggy play time into your walk or run.

DELAVEAGA PARK: Another popular park for dogs. They are allowed on many of the trails, but not on the athletic fields.

SAN LORENZO RIVER LEVEE: The wide and often quiet path along the river makes for a nice walk or run with your dog.

How Far Can a Dog Run?

How far a dog can run depends on many factors, including the dog's body type, breed, and overall physical condition. Dogs (like people!) that haven't been running regularly need to start out slowly and build up. Always check with your veterinarian if you have any questions about your dog's ability as a running companion.

Respect Your Dog's Limits (Even If Your Dog Doesn't!)

Many dogs will follow their people long past their limits, continuing even when they are exhausted or hurt. In addition, a dog running off leash will often go ahead or take "side trips" into the woods, adding a lot of extra distance to the run or walk. Training dogs to run with you or keeping them on leash (as is required in most places) can help you ensure your dog doesn't overdo.

Safety

When exercising, dogs may need two to three times the amount of water as normal.

Avoid exercising your dog in the heat of the day. If it is hot, keep him or her cooler by wetting him down. Use caution in the cold too. Dogs with short fur may be especially vulnerable.

Running or walking over rough or hot surfaces can be tough on a dog's pads, causing them to tear or wear through. Dogs are also susceptible to strain on their joints and bones from running on hard surfaces.

Other Things You Should Know

Puppies under a year should not run long distances. Their joints are not fully formed until they are at least a year old (a year and a half for large breed dogs) and repetitive exercise like running can damage the joints as they are forming.

Many veterinarians recommend avoiding exercise for one hour before and two hours after meals to help prevent bloat.

RUNNING OR WALKING ON TRACKS

UCSC

UCSC has a half-mile track behind the West Field House. Though not a typical 400-meter track, it is a paved, flat loop with a spectacular view of the Monterey Bay and Santa Cruz Mountains. The surface is a combination of asphalt and softer macadam (tar and gravel). It loops around a large, grassy field which is sometimes used for soccer, rugby, ultimate Frisbee, volleyball and softball. There is one small hill on this loop. UCSC requires a parking permit or parking at metered spaces. There are some metered spaces at the West Field House lot.

Santa Cruz High, Harbor High and Cabrillo College

Both high schools and Cabrillo College have a 400-meter dirt track. While better than pavement for your joints, the dirt can be rutted, uneven and hard-packed. During the rainy season they are usually muddy and full of puddles. During the spring track season, these tracks are better maintained. Parking is available on the neighborhood streets and at Harbor High School and Cabrillo College in the parking lots. Parking is very difficult at Cabrillo College when school is in session.

Soquel and Aptos High School

Soquel and Aptos High School have all-weather tracks. These are 400-meter tracks with a world class rubberized surface. Both of these tracks were built with funds from the Wharf to Wharf race and from community fundraising efforts. The all-weather surface is very forgiving and easy on your body. It is also very fast and your times will be faster than on trails or the roads. Drainage is very good and there are seldom puddles, but the tracks can be slippery when wet. Parking is available after-hours in the school parking lots.

Although these tracks are widely used by the community, their use is at the discretion of the host school. It is best to restrict your use to non-school hours.

Benefits of Using a Track

Running or walking on a measured track can be very beneficial in a fitness program. Many people prefer to know exactly how far they are going, and a measured track is extremely accurate. The softness of the surface is easy on your joints, and you can keep a consistent rhythm and pace. Your attention can really wander since there are no streets to cross or roots to jump over. Tracks are usually completely flat for those who prefer not to encounter hills.

Tracks can also help parents of young children keep fit. You can bring your children to the track and allow them to play on the grass or enjoy the sand of the long-jump pits while you run. Children remain within your supervision but you can still run or walk at your pace.

In Santa Cruz County we are fortunate to have a selection of tracks from which to choose.

TREADMILL RUNNING AT SANTA CRUZ GYMS

Despite all the beautiful places in Santa Cruz to run, there may be times when you want to run indoors. If you are not comfortable running in the rain or in winter darkness, running on a treadmill in a gym can be a dry and bright respite. If you want to do precise and measured workouts, with feedback on exactly how far and how fast you are running, most treadmills will provide that information as you run. Some people like the motivation that the forced pacing of a treadmill demands. Most gyms in Santa Cruz also provide an opportunity for cross-training on a variety of cardiovascular equipment, a good way to get an extra cardiovascular workout on a non-running day and a good alternative if you are recovering from a running injury and need a non-impact exercise routine.

Santa Cruz has many good gyms with treadmills and other cardiovascular equipment. Check the phone book's yellow pages directory for current listings.

Chris Clark, a 2000 Olympian, did almost all of her serious training on a treadmill. A virtually unknown runner, Clark surprised the running world by winning the 2000 US Women's Olympic Marathon Trials. She credits her victory to the use of a treadmill in her training. A pathologist and mother of two, Clark resides in Alaska where the roads remain snow-covered virtually all winter. Out of necessity she trained on a treadmill. She said the treadmill kept her honest. You cannot exaggerate your pace when the machine is set. She also believes running indoors inadvertently helped her acclimate to the unexpected 75-degree heat in South Carolina on the day of the race.

RUNNING SAFETY TIPS

Consult your doctor before beginning a running or walking program.

As with any physical activity, you should first consult your health care professional before beginning a running or walking program. Once you have worked up to a few miles, you can enjoy any of the runs in this book if you keep a few safety tips in mind.

Always warm up and cool down.

Slow jogging or walking before your run allows your heart to adjust to the demand of running. It also allows your muscles to get warm and loose. Similarly, slow jogging or walking when you are finished allows your heart to return gradually to its normal rate and your body to cool off.

Always let someone know where you are planning to run if you will be alone.

This is especially important on trail runs.

Carry identification.

If you do run alone, carry identification and consider carrying a cell phone with you.

Poison oak treatment.

After running on trails where poison oak is present, wash with a cleansing treatment such as Tecnu. This product can be purchased in most drug stores. When used according to the directions, it can be very helpful in removing the oils that cause the itchy rash associated with poison oak. Be sure to wash exposed clothing as well.

When running at night, wear reflective clothing.

No matter how well you can see the cars, they cannot see you without reflective clothing and shoes.

Good quality running shoes are essential.

Buy your shoes from reputable sports shops or running specialty stores, which usually have qualified sales people to assist you. Make sure you get a good fit. Running shoes should feel comfortable as soon as you try them on. They do not need to be broken in. Be sure you try on shoes late in the day when your feet have swelled. A good rule of thumb is to have one fingernail width at the toe. This will help prevent your shoes from feeling too tight a few miles into your run.

Treating injuries.

If you do sustain an injury, seek out a health care professional who is familiar with running injuries. They will best be able to understand your injury.

Other Things You Should Know

Mountain lions

Mountain lions have been sighted occasionally in the parks and on the trails of Santa Cruz County. If you encounter a mountain lion, do not run. Stand tall, open your jacket, and make yourself look as big as possible. Do not crouch down or bend over. Raise your hands in the air, or if you can, pick up a big stick and wave it high the air. Do not take your eyes off the mountain lion. If you are with a small child, hold the child up in the air above you. Slowly back away. Do not turn your back on the mountain lion.

PACE CHART

The chart below will help you determine your "pace per mile." If you know how far you have run, look in the row that shows how long it took you to run that distance to determine your "pace per mile." If you have a goal to run at a certain pace, you can look across the row to see in what amount of time you will need to run the various distances listed in order to meet that pace.

If You Run This Far:					
2 miles	3 miles	5 km	5 miles	10 km	Your Pace Per Mile
24:00	36:00	37:17	1:00:00	1:14:34	12:00
23:00	34:30	35:44	57:30	1:11:27	11:30
22:00	33:00	34:11	55:00	1:08:21	11:00
21:00	31:30	32:37	52:30	1:05:15	10:30
20:00	30:00	31:04	50:00	1:02:08	10:00
19:30	29:15	30:18	48:45	1:00:35	9:45
19:00	28:30	29:31	47:30	59:02	9:30
18:30	27:45	28:44	46:15	57:29	9:15
18:00	27:00	27:58	45:00	55:55	9:00
17:30	26:15	27:11	43:45	54:22	8:45
17:00	25:30	26:24	42:30	52:49	8:30
16:30	24:45	25:38	41:15	51:16	8:15
16:00	24:00	24:51	40:00	49:43	8:00
15:30	23:15	24:05	38:45	48:09	7:45
15:00	22:30	23:18	37:30	46:36	7:30
14:30	21:45	22:31	36:15	45:03	7:15
14:00	21:00	21:45	35:00	43:30	7:00
13:30	20:15	20:58	33:45	41:57	6:45
13:00	19:30	20:12	32:30	40:23	6:30
12:30	18:45	19:25	31:15	38:50	6:15
12:00	18:00	18:38	30:00	37:17	6:00
11:30	17:15	17:52	28:45	35:44	5:45
11:00	16:30	17:05	27:30	34:11	5:30
10:30	15:45	16:19	26:15	32:37	5:15
10:00	15:00	15:32	25:00	31:04	5:00
9:30	14:15	14:45	23:45	29:31	4:45

In This Amount of Time:

This is Your Pace Per Mile:

RESOURCES
. . . .

The Santa Cruz Track Club
www.sctc.runners.net

City of Santa Cruz Department of Parks and Recreation
323 Church St.
Santa Cruz, CA 95060
831 420-5250
www.ci.santa-cruz.ca.us/pr/parksrec/

Santa Cruz County Department of Parks, Open Space and Cultural Services
979 17th Ave.
Santa Cruz, CA 95062
www.scparks.com

California State Parks
Pajaro Coast Division
144 School St
Santa Cruz, CA 95060-3726
831 429-2850
www.parks.ca.gov

Friends of Santa Cruz State Parks
144 School St.
Santa Cruz, CA 95060
831 429-1840
www.scparkfriends.org

The Advocates For Nisene Marks State Park
P.O. Box 461
Aptos, CA 95001-0461

VirtualParks.org
Developed by Erik Goetze, VirtualParks.org is a wonderful website that not only presents 360 degree photographic panoramas from wilderness sites throughout the world (including Santa Cruz), but also colorful and detailed maps of many parks within Santa Cruz County.

YOUR ROUTE CHECKLIST AND LOG

If you run or walk every route described in this book you will have traveled approximately 235 miles and you will have an intimate knowledge of Santa Cruz far beyond that of most locals. To help you keep track of your efforts, we have listed all the routes as they appear in the book. Every time you finish one of the routes, check it off, mark the date, and feel good about your accomplishment.

NEIGHBORHOOD ROUTES	DISTANCE	DATE COMPLETED
❏ West Cliff Drive	5 miles	_____
❏ University Terrace/Arroyo Seco Canyon Trail Loop	2.5 miles	_____
❏ Upper Westside Neighborhood Loops		
☐ Escalona/King Street Loop	2.3 miles	_____
☐ High Street Loop	3 miles	_____
❏ Downtown Santa Cruz Neighborhood Loop	5 miles	_____
❏ San Lorenzo River Levee	4.7 miles	_____
❏ Seabright Neighborhood Loop	3 miles	_____
❏ Prospect Heights Neighborhood Loop	3.3 miles	_____
❏ Santa Cruz Yacht Harbor	3.8 miles	_____
❏ Pleasure Point and Moran Lake	2.4 miles	_____
❏ Capitola/Soquel Creek Loop	1.6 miles	_____
❏ Rio Del Mar Loop	3.1 miles	_____

PARKS AND GREENBELT	DISTANCE	DATE COMPLETED
❏ Wilder Ranch State Park: The Bluffs		
☐ Old Cove Landing Trail	2–2.5 miles	_____
☐ Ohlone Bluff Trail	7 miles	_____
❏ Wilder Ranch State Park: The Backcountry		
☐ Englesman Loop Trail	3.1 miles	_____
☐ Wilder Ridge Trail Loop	6.9 miles	_____
☐ Eucalyptus Loop	7.6 miles	_____
☐ Enchanted Loop Trail	1.6 miles	_____
☐ Long Meadow Loop	5.8 miles	_____
❏ Moore Creek Preserve		
☐ Prairie View/Terrace Loop Trail	2.4 miles	_____
☐ Moore Creek Trail	2.6 miles	_____
❏ UCSC Campus Natural Preserve		
☐ Chinquapin Road	4.4 miles	_____
☐ Alternative Loops	1–2 miles	_____
❏ Natural Bridges State Beach and Antonelli Pond	1.3–2.1 miles	_____
❏ Henry Cowell Redwoods State Park: Highway 9 Entrance		
☐ Redwood Grove Loop Trail	.8 miles	_____
☐ River Trail Loop	2.5 miles	_____
☐ Eagle Creek Loop	4.6 miles	_____
❏ Henry Cowell Redwoods State Park: Graham Hill Entrance		
☐ Graham Hill Loop	3.6 miles	_____
☐ Pine Trial Loop	5.6 miles	_____

PARKS AND GREENBELT (CONTINUED)	DISTANCE	DATE COMPLETED
☐ **Fall Creek**		
☐ Trail to Lime Kilns	2.4 miles	_____
☐ Trail to Barrel Mill Site	5.2 miles	_____
☐ Big Ben Loop Trail	8.1 miles	_____
☐ **Upper Pogonip: Spring Street Entrance**		
☐ Spring and Rincon Trail	3.4 miles	_____
☐ Lime Kiln and Spring Box Trail Loop	3.2 miles	_____
☐ Lookout Trail Loop	3.1 miles	_____
☐ **Lower Pogonip: Harvey West Park Entrance**		
☐ Pogonip Creek Nature Trail	2.8 miles	_____
☐ Fern Trail Loop	4.6 miles	_____
☐ **DeLaveaga Park**		
☐ Lower Loop	1.3 miles	_____
☐ Top of the World Trail	3 miles	_____
☐ Sand Pit Road	2 miles	_____
☐ **Schwan Lake Park**	1.1 miles	_____
☐ **Anna Jean Cummings Park**		
☐ Jogging and Walking Path	.5 miles	_____
☐ Killer Hill Trail	.8 miles	_____
☐ **The Forest of Nisene Marks: The Lower Trails**		
☐ George's Picnic Area Loop	2.6 miles	_____
☐ Old Growth Loop	1.5 miles	_____
☐ **The Forest of Nisene Marks: The Upper Trail**		
☐ West Ridge Trail Loop	8.4 miles	_____
☐ Sandpoint via the West Ridge Trail or Hoffman's	11.4–13.4 miles	_____
☐ Mill Pond Trail	1.6 miles	_____
☐ Bridge Creek Trail	6 miles	_____
☐ Aptos Creek Trail	10.5–11.9 miles	_____
☐ **Santa Cruz County Beaches**		
☐ Santa Cruz Beach and Cowells Beach	.2–.6 miles	_____
☐ Seabright Beach	.5 miles	_____
☐ Twin Lakes Beach	.3 miles	_____
☐ New Brighton and Seacliff Beaches	3.3 miles	_____

POPULAR RACE ROUTES	DISTANCE	DATE COMPLETED
☐ **Wharf to Wharf**	6 miles	_____
☐ **Turkey Trot and Super Bowl Run**	"1K, 5K, 10K"	_____
☐ **Firecracker 10K**	10K	
☐ **UCSC Slug Run**	5K–10K	_____
☐ **Aptos Women's 5-Miler**	5 miles	_____
☐ **Cardiac Pacer**	5 miles	_____

ROUTE PAGE INDEX

ABOUT THE AUTHORS

Eileen Brown

Eileen Brown began running on the trails and roads of upstate New York while a student at SUNY Binghamton. She continued her love of running and became an elite competitive runner after moving to Santa Cruz in 1984. She competed in two Olympic Trials in the marathon with a personal best of 2:40:51.

Steven Bignell

Steven Bignell has been running off and on since his freshman year at UCSC over 35 years ago, never very fast or very far. After his son joined the Santa Cruz Track Club Youth Cross Country team, Steven found himself getting consistently outrun by an 11-year-old and decided he had better start running more regularly. Since he likes to know how far he has run (or maybe not), he thought this would be a good idea for a book. Steven is a longtime health educator and the publisher at Journeyworks.

NOTES

NOTES

ORDER FORM TO PURCHASE EXTRA COPIES FOR FRIENDS, FAMILY AND COLLEAGUES.

If you can't locate a copy of this book at your bookstore or other retailer, you are welcome to order it directly from Journeyworks.

Please send me_____copies of **Santa Cruz: A Guide for Runners, Joggers and Serious Walkers** @$12.95 per copy.

Name_____

Address_____

City_____

State_____

Zip_____

Telephone (daytime)_____

Email_____

Quantity_____ (x $12.95) = $_____

CA sales tax at $1.07 per book $_____

Shipping ($3.00 for first book and 75¢ for each additional book) $_____

Total: $_____

Enclose a check or Money Order payable to Journeyworks Publishing

Or charge to this credit card: ❏ VISA   ❏ MasterCard

Credit Card Number_____

Expiration Date_____

Name_____
(please print exactly as it appears on card)

Signature_____

Send your order to:
Journeyworks Publishing
P.O. Box 8466
Santa Cruz, CA 95061-8466

Books can also be ordered via phone with a credit card by calling 831-423-1400 during business hours (M–F 8:30 a.m. to 4:30 p.m.).